And now all this

Your thanks are due to the Vice-Proctor of the Hole Pocket University for insisting on the bathing costumes; and to Mr. John Reynolds for kindly leaving this Maddening Symbolical Design unfinished.

And now all this

By the authors of
1066 AND ALL THAT

Being Vol. I of the Hole Pocket Treasury
of Absolutely General Knowledge

IN X CONSOLING SECTIONS,
WITH NUMEROUS MEMORABLE DIAGRAMS,
1 ANAGRAM, 2 TEST PAPERS (BAD LUCK), 3 RELIEF MAPS,
SEVERAL POUNDS OF *FIGS*,
ONLY 5 APPENDIXES, NO INDEXES,
OR DEDICATIONS (BRAVO), VERY FEW NOTES,
THREE RHYMES
AND PRACTICALLY NO REASONS GIVEN

Absolutely General Editors

W. C. SELLAR

And

R. J. YEATMAN

Director of Illustrations

JOHN REYNOLDS

METHUEN

Published by Methuen 1999

1 3 5 7 9 10 8 6 4 2

First published in the United Kingdom in 1932 by Methuen & Co Ltd

This edition published in 1999 by
Methuen Publishing Limited
215 Vauxhall Bridge Road, London SW1V 1EJ

Peribo Pty Ltd, 58 Beaumont Road, Mount Kuring-Gai
NSW 2080, Australia, ACN 002 273 761
(for Australia and New Zealand)

Copyright © 1932 by W.C. Sellar and R.J. Yeatman

Methuen Publishing Limited Reg. No. 3543167

A CIP catalogue record for this book is available from the British Library

ISBN 0 413 77380 9

Authors' Impressions
First Impression, January 1932 . . . A Good Thing
Second Impression, August 1932 . . . A Bad Thing
Third Impression, October 1932 . . . Anything you Say

Printed and bound in the United Kingdom by
Cox & Wyman Ltd, Reading Berkshire

Papers used by Methuen Publishing Limited are natural, recycable
products made from wood grown in sustainable forests. The manufacturing
processes conform to enviromental regulations of the country of origin.

CONTENTS

AUTHORS' NOTE

SEVERAL Portions of this book have appeared in *Punch*, and two in *The Daily Mail*, and are reprinted here by courtesy of the Proprietors of those papers.

ERRATUM

Chap I.   *For* Ginger beard *eat* Ginger-bread *throughout*.

INTRODUCTION

ABOUT ALL YOU KNOW

EVERY SCHOOLMASTER KNOWS that for every one person who wants to teach there are approximately 30 who don't want to learn—much.

In fact, the Sad Thing about Education is that *nobody loves it—much*. (Bad luck.)

This has been the chief Educational Problem for the past two or three hundred or thousand (say, hundred thousand) years, and it sometimes surprises the authors to think how easily they solved it. (Don't mention it.)

The Truth is—*Education is no good unless you know it*. The rest is just Useless Knowledge.

In a previous Work the authors demonstrated that History was not what people thought—but what they could remember.*

An extension of this principle is urgently necessary if the whole of Education is not to fall into disrepute, and be abandoned like The Use of The Globes and The Dates of The Kings of Israel and Judah.

We therefore now lay down the further revolutionary, but unanswerable and utterly consoling, principle—namely, that since Knowledge is not palatable unless you know it there is no room in a general education for anything except Absolutely General Knowledge.

* See Compulsory Preface to " 1066 And All That."

Vol. I of the Hole Pocket Treasury of Absolutely General Knowledge is only a beginning : the authors are aware that they have undertaken a life-work (fortunately they are fairly old)—no less a task than *to teach everybody everything everybody knows*.

This book is naturally the result of the most stupendous researches, in the course of which the authors spared no one, not even themselves. For instance, in order to do Section III (Psycho-Babycraft) they went to the length of tossing up—the loser marrying, having the baby, etc., thus leaving the winner free to develop the Infantile Psychology.

They also borrowed a number of rare Birds, and watched them migrate, Knitted a ten-foot sock, examined some professional classes on Ancient Lore and extracted a large amount of myth-information (especially from stock-brokers) ; and finally (to test the generally-accepted theories of health- and body-culture) consumed fabulous quantities of Vitamins, Roughage, Cabbage and other Garbage.

In our first educational work we congratulated everyone on the fact that History was at an end. Vol. I of the Hole Pocket Treasury signalises the fact that *Education has begun afresh,* and that this time you will All be Top at Everything.

This volume, then, will tell you, so far as its scope extends, about All You Know, and you will be surprised to find *how little you have to learn*.

All This is really very consoling . . . at least, we hope so.

I

AN OUTLINE OF BODICURE

CHAPTER I

MIND AND BODY

" *MOST people eat too much, too often, too fast, too long, too loud, and too little. This is a great mistake.*"

(Page 2, Third Alimentary Tract, pub. by H.M. Commission on Girth Control.)

The mistake is chiefly felt, as is generally known, in the *body*, which to quote the Tract again, " suffers distension, distortion disillusion and finally explosion."
Bad luck

But there is an even worse mistake   most people go through life eating *the wrong food*   The effect is disastrous . imperceptibly, ignominiously, but inevitably they become *the wrong people*.

This must, of course, be due to the effect of food on the human *mind*.

But here a tremendous difficulty arises. As Cézanne first pointed out, *it is impossible to draw a hard and fast line between the Mind and the Body.*

It is quite true. You can't do it. The fact is, as Cézanne would have put it, " *Cependant vite . . .* " or

more probably " Qu'elle que soit la vitesse avec quoi
. . . " or more probably not ; anyway, THE FACT
REMAINS, that however fast (or hard) you draw THE
RESULT IS ALWAYS A CLERGYMAN (see fig. 1).

Fig. 1.

CHAPTER II

LIKE THE ANIMALS

MAN has evolved from the lower animal creation.

This is, of course, unnatural. If Man is to be Healthy
in the highest sense, he must give up all evolution in
unnatural directions. He must break clean away from
all *sedentary occupations*, such as sitting down, taking
the chair, etc., and GET ON ALL FOURS WITH NATURE.

He must learn to sleep head-downwards like the
bats ; to talk less and scratch more ; to rattle his skin

about like a horse, or snap out of it altogether like a snake. . . .

Woman, too, has much to learn : for instance, she

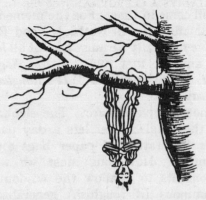

must learn to build her own nest, and lay her own eggs in it ; she must dress in brown, even in the mating season, and follow the male in docile herds . . . but be prepared, like the insects, to exterminate the husband the moment he begins to *Drone*.

It is the only way.

CHAPTER III

EAT MORE JUTE

ALL that will come in time. For the moment, the only hope for humanity lies in Ruthless Food Reform. If Man is to live naturally he must first of all learn to eat (naturally) and the first rule is :—*Roughage first and last—in fact, as Browning said, " It's Roughage, Roughage all the way."*

You cannot deceive Nature. The elephant, wisest denizen of the jungle, never lets a day pass without exacting its full ration of paper bags and woollen Tam-'o-shanters. How long must we wait before mankind consents to swallow the wisdom of Kurapotkin's luminous (if roughish) generalisation that *" There is more food value in one black béret than in one hundred-weight of blackberries " ?*

Fig. 11

Again, take the question of Stimulants and Narcotics. These were, of course, originally intended by Nature for use *with a doctor's certificate only* (bad luck). Yet Man continues to jeopardise his future with alcohol and protocol, caffein and protein, nicotine and seccotine, tannin, tiffin, and even tocsin (which is now known to be nothing more nor less than pure poison !).

When, as everybody knows nowadays, what the body requires is *Vitamins*, Calories, Celeries, Fritillaries, Phagocytes, and *of course Phosphates*.

IT HAS DEFINITELY BEEN PROVED THAT LACK OF PHOSPHATES PRODUCES PHACESPHOTS (see fig. 11).

CHAPTER IV

RADICAL FOOD REFORM

THERE is only one way of securing the right Vitamins and Phosphates and that is to ingest the right food, thus becoming, probably, the *right person* (Safety First, see Chap. I).

What does this amount to ?

As a matter of fact, it amounts to practically nothing (except, of course, Roughage), since " *it is essential to avoid all soups, fish-dishes, entrées, joints, sweets and savoures* "—to say nothing of *sundries* :—the fact is, it is now practically General Knowledge that COOKING transforms food from a Harmless Evil into a FATAL DRUG.

Man's *natural* foods (such as raw roots, red rugs,

black bérets, and Grade A Tuberculin-free cokernuts) are all intended by nature to be eaten whole and, of course, raw, the vitamins which they contain being mostly concentrated in the hair which grows on the outer surface, or rind.

Take the typical CASE OF TANGERINES. The really

valuable part is the *skin*, and, of course, the silver paper ; while most beneficial of all is, perhaps, the splendid natural ungranulated crate itself. And yet there are thousands of people who quite casually hack off all this invaluable *casein* and *throw it away*!

CHAPTER V

SOME RADICAL RECIPES

THERE is only one reservation : although it is quite certain that all cooking (and eating, too, for that matter) must eventually be discarded altogether, some Food Reformers are prepared to countenance (temporarily) certain forms of strictly "*Conservative*" Cooking. But this is already out-of-date : *Radical Cookery* is (temporarily) the Thing of the Moment.

A few examples of the latter may therefore be given —without fear or flavour, but with the proviso that the authors accept no responsibility for anything that may or may not result.

I. TO BAKE (RADICALLY) ENOUGH HOME-MADE GINGER BEARD FOR ONE PERSON.

Take as much flour and water as you think you will Knead.

Need it desperately with both Knees.

Yeast and ginger are now easily worked in, *but remember that yeast is yeast and that the Beard will never rise unless you work desperately away from the waistcoat.*

Now Kneal down and obtrude the Beard unobtrusively into the oven.

Close the oven door sharply, with a soft bang.

Presently you will feel the Beard rising (with bearded bubbles winking at the brim).

Keep cool for 2 hours, pricking occasionally against the kick to see if Beard has risen to occasion.

When the Beard explodes, withdraw guiltily, roll quickly into a demi-whorl or *croissant* and decorate with ratafia, latakia, or raffia-work to taste, toast, etc.

Stroke gingerly (frowning a little perhaps) until the guilt is off. . . .

2. AN AMUSING LITTLE SANDWICH TO THROW OUT OF A RAILWAY CARRIAGE.

Take a conservative school-capful of fresh dandelion's milk.

Add butter to size and prepare pestles, trench-mortars, etc.

Batter to bits in the buttery, or vice versa.

Spread the batter over a whole-mill stone, and fold the latter, once.

Hang this festive little sandwich round your neck, and throw yourself well clear of the foot-board as train passes over Forth Bridge.

CHAPTER VI

THERE'S ALWAYS TO-MORROW

WE shall have failed entirely in our object if the Reader, after making trial of the above recipes, should run away with the idea that Reformed Feeding is either dull or monotonous.

On the contrary, there are hundreds of interesting

little luncheon recipes which require nothing but a pinch of hunger and a soupçon of one-o'clock courage.

We append therefore a schedule of distracting little *préparations* for each day of the week.

SUNDAE

The day of Meditation ; should, strictly, be devoted to Food for Thought and other spiritual nutriment : the following recipe may, however, prove edifying if not materially speaking, edible.

New leaf Turn-over

Take a new leaf (tea, tea-rose or tea-cabbage, to teaste).

Turn it over meditatively in the mind's eye.

Close the eye,

definitely,

till——

MONDAE

Banana Surprise

Take one sweet, black, over-ripe banana

Make a slit in the outer tubing.

Gut the banana.

Stuff with cotton-wool, sew up tightly and serve scar downwards.

TUESDAE

Tangerine Tour de Force

Order a crate of tangerines.

Make hole in crate.

Swallow hole.

WEDNESDAE
Date Pudding
(Suitable for any day of the year)

Take 2 home-made figs.

Drop them on the floor probably.

Take 2 fresh home-made figs.

Hold on tight.

Now take a conservatively-edited hard-boiled newspaper and cut out the date.

Sprinkle with favour of prox or ultimo and add figs to date.

Thanking you in anticipation,

Yours through a straw, darkly. . . .

THURSDAE
Treacle Pullover

Take a handful of unsweetened black treacle.

Inflate to 99% over an open flame.

Add 222 tblspnsfuls, or one ½ chstfdrsfl, of bswx.

Pull it about for an hour or two on strong string.

If still at a loose end *pull it right over your head from behind* and serve you right.

FRIDAE
Brown Paper Dainties

Take 2 thick ripe brown-paper parcels.

Bang them together till exhausted

Ring up old college chum and invite to lunch.

NOTE : Be careful to invite self to lunch, not chum

Whole Meal Biscuit

Unfold table napkin.

Take up biscuit (*if ginger, gingerly*).

Swallow biscuit.

Fold table napkin, hands, etc., and wait patiently for next meal.

If unable to wait, attempt radically to swallow napkin, hands, etc.

Diddle Dumpling

(*A Laughable Little Sundry for April 1st or other Bogus Centenaries.*)

We include this rather heartless little *ventre-plat* chiefly on account of its being so enervatingly easy. There is, in fact, as you must have guessed, nothing in it.

Having obtained an ounce or two of Dumpling Powder, you just—

Think of a number,

Dumple it,

Take away the number you first thought of,

Serve the Dumpling (dimpling slightly) to famished gangsters. . . .

And don't blame us if they start *bumpling you off*.

NUTRITIOUS SAYINGS

" Always get up from the table feeling as if you couldn't eat another mouthful." *Prof. Roughage.*

" I hold out no hope for the confirmed food addict " *Prof. Rumble.*

" Always get up from the table." *Sir Chas. Addict.*
" If the Doctor's away, send for a well-known apple."
A Medical Practitioner.

" One meal a day is ample and one day to a meal the
ideal to aim at." *New York Culinary Digest.*

"Alimentary, my dear Watson." *S. Holmes (passim.)*

BIBLIOGRAPHY OF HEALTH-CRAFT AND BODICURE

Stones of Venice . . . by Professor Ruskage
Off the Beeton Track . . by Knut Kutlut (trans. from the Swedish by Hamish McSandwish)

Cookery Nook . . . by Mary Broughage
On All Fours with Nature . by A. Rabbit

Read also :—

FOOD, ETC.

The Scarlet Pumpernickel . by The Baroness Orgy
The Bending of A Fig . . by Lady ffig-Bendish
Memoirs of the Count de Bortsch
Underdones of War . . by A Battery Cook

PHYSIQUE, ETC.

The Daly Dozen . . . by (the late) George Edwardes

Also, for *Dangerous Indian Dishes* :—

My Kukri Book . . . by The Ham Sahib of Sickim

THEORY AND PRACTICE OF POLAR EXPLORATION

A Brief Manual for Modern Pole-Crashers

I. INTRODUCTION

THERE are three sorts of Pole ; the North Pole, the South Pole, and the Boy Scout's or Baden Pole. . . . Read on with Arctic calm ; worse hardships are in store . . .

II. OBJECT OF MODERN EXPLORATION

Almost every year spectacular dashes to the Poles are made by Submarine, Supermarine, Soup-tureen and, of course, by Underground (it's cooler) ; but we must warn you in advance that the idea of discovering where the Poles are is absolutely *démodé*, because it is now absolutely General Knowledge that the North Pole is right at the top and that the South Pole is quite all right at the bottom. Indeed, the positions of these particular poles are now actually *visible*, as anyone can verify by ascending to the top landing of the Eiffel Tower on a day when visibility is good and opening the Atlas at the right page (try page 3).

No, the object of all Modern Exploration is, of course, to lecture with a terrific cinema film when you get back.

You will therefore be concerned mainly with undergoing every describable hardship and suffering the most terrible conditions available.

With a little forethought, however, you should be able to experience all that any film audience can reasonably expect in the way of sufferings and miseries, including the cold (terrific, they say) and the various kinds of painful polar Ice, such as *hummock ice* (which holds explorers up for days), *hammock ice* (which lets them down at nights) and the dangerous *stomach ice* (which causes the frozen waists on which so many explorers perish).

On no account miss the Dreadful Polar Night, which is equally dreadful whichever Pole you attempt, inasmuch as it is dark all the year round and bright all night at the North Pole, while in summer it is light all the year round and pitch-dark all day at the South Pole.

In addition you will find that there is no latitude or longitude at the Poles or any of the usual Geographical comforts and that you will be in continuous danger of being sucked down into the vortex of the dreadful Aurora Borealis.

NOTE : Specimens of all these things including Polar Walri, Pola Negri, etc., are now kept at the film studios ; so there will be no need for you actually to take any Polar films till you get back to London.

III. BYRD LIFE, ETC.

Apart from the howling buzzards which buffet all explorers impartially, you will encounter mountain penguins, fountain penguins and many other strange beasts including the terrible Igloo, which feed on fish, explorers, and even etcetera.

To protect himself against these the explorer should adopt Nature's wonderful device of protective colouring and clothe himself in white (as the polar bears do to guard themselves against the assaults of seals, seagulls, scakale, etc.), thus achieving complete immunity or *nunatak* as we old explorers call it.

IV. CLOTHING AND OTHER EQUIPMENT

Inexpensive Polar Outfits can now be obtained at most of the leading London Stores. All clothing should of course be air-tight ; and, if possible, bear-tight, too.

But in addition to your unshrinkable thermos boots, and unthinkable walrus-hide handkerchiefs and so on you will undoubtedly require some *Companions*.

Choose your companions carefully, you may have to eat them. . . .

V. POLAR BEARINGS

American audiences in particular are terrifically keen on *facts*, so start with a clear idea *which pole* you are dashing at, and try to start *facing the right way*. Conditions at the Poles are deceptively similar and the compass will not help you, since, though one end of the compass notoriously points to the N. Pole and the other to the S. Pole, there is nothing on the compass to show *which end is which* (bad luck).

Furthermore, the Pole being a purely imaginary erection, there will be *nothing there*, except you, when you arrive, and the accompanying map of the district will be of no assistance to you whatever.

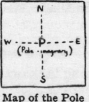

Map of the Pole
and environs

Tear up the map, therefore, along the dotted line, and work your compass to a standstill : if it then points straight up you will know you are at the N. Pole ; if it points straight downwards you are at the S. Pole, and *vice versa*. (N.B. If you appear to be at the wrong Pole you might try holding the compass upside down.)

But in any case you are not at the real Pole, yet. A glance at your geography book will remind you that the compass will have only led you to the Magnetic

Pole, and that you are still about 1,000 miles from THE POLE itself. (*Jolly bad luck.*)

Now is the time to start eating your companions.

Begin with the smallest and work upwards towards yourself. Be sure to leave yourself till last.

Begin with the smallest

VI. ETIQUETTE

If you decide to bring back one of your companions as a souvenir (or perhaps as a joke), do not allow him to mingle too much with the animal life. Quite serious family complications arose recently owing to a certain leader *bringing back a penguin by mistake*.

Bringing back a companion may involve eating instead a certain amount of *pummican*, the well-known explorers' food which is made of pelicanised friable pumice-stones and which can be mentioned miserably in your lectures if you get hard up for hardships.

The proper etiquette, by the way, when meeting a penguin to which you have not previously been introduced, is to doff your panama and remark, deferentially,

" Dr. Livingstone, I presume . . ." This never fails to break the ice.

One more word about the penguins. Do not let them embarrass you if they happen to drop in when you are just sitting down to dinner. Evening dress is quite optional in Arctic Circles.

CONCLUSION

If you follow the foregoing hints with reasonable care and avoid romping with the polar bears (which causes frost-bite) or snow-balling with your companions which, as is generally known, often brings on a form of temporary snow-blindness, you should have little difficulty in getting to at least one of the Poles in record time in a bath-chair, or dumb-waiter, or other hitherto unattempted vehicle, and becoming a dreadful Polar Knight yourself and writing a manual of your own.

But you had better do it soon : there is, we understand, a well-supported movement to close the Arctic Circles after eight o'clock and to prohibit Sunday exploration altogether.

III

PSYCHO-BABYCRAFT

*A Guide to Mental Hygiene—for Modern Babies
Between the Ages of 0 and 3*

CHAPTER I

THE OPEN MIND

AS expert psycho-anomalists and Professional Happy Mediums, the authors would be the last to deny that the main object of Modern Psychology is *to catch people out*—to surprise persons (or even parsons) secretly adoring their boot-trees, suppressing their terrors, pressing their trousers, or *even worse* . . .

Unfortunately, the tendency is *to catch the people too late ;* psychologists have themselves, till now, psubconsciously phunked the phact that it is not only their duty to catch people but to *catch them young.*

This Manual is designed therefore for use by NORMAL PRE-ADULTS BETWEEN THE AGES OF 0 AND 3—"*the only persons whose minds, being as yet uncontaminated by inhibitions, aspirations, aspirins, hymns (ancient or modern), travelogues, decalogues or even logarithms, are still Open to Reason.*" (Muggmeister.)

Still open to reason

At this point the Reader will doubtless become the prey of an irresistible desire (or Libido) to know the answer to the totally frightful question—" Is there still some hope for Me ? "

Well, you will just have to resist it. Before we can tell you the answer, we must ask you to decide the utterly fraughtful question—*ARE YOU A BABY?*

HOW TO TELL

Method A. Observation.

It is more difficult than you might think. But we will begin with a simple case. (Don't mention it.)

As you know, *babies have no teeth at all*. Good : you are sitting in front of the fire, without any teeth, but you have a long whitish beard and *whiskers which crackle to the touch*. Are you a Baby ? The anwers is —No. You are probably your grandfather.

Now let us take a more difficult case. Babies (but not grandfathers) are very fond of milk. Now then : you are sitting in front of the fire, feeling very satisfied because you have just had some milk. You have a long bushy tail and whiskers which *do not crackle at all* (bad luck).

Are you a Baby ?

The answer is " No," again. You are, though you may not know it, The Cat.

Again, if you are bald, or " thin on top," you may or may not be a Baby. Some are and some aren't. So be careful.

But you must decide. There is no time to lose. As Hoggmeister says—" The education of young babies begins *in very early youth.*" Have a good look at the bathroom. And the bedroom, too. If they have recently become pharmaceutical museums full of cotton-wool, woollen cots, piffs, puffs, poofs, and lids of pink celluloid recepticules, then there can be no doubt about it. *There is a baby somewhere in the house.*

The only question is—*Is it You ?*

Method B. Introspection.

Now is the time to try the introspective method, viz. auto-analysis. If after a critical and exhaustive introspection you decide that you have no teeth, whiskers, tail or tobacco-pouch, and are simply a helpless bundle of blankets, biblets, driblets, pilch-bockers and Kidknappies—then you can't get away from the fact—You are It.

You are ? Bravo ! Take your fist out of your mouth

and try to take in

CHAPTER II

WHAT EVERY BABY KNOWS

HAVING established your status, you must impose yourself. Frustration, at your age, is fatal. *You must have it all your own way*.

Otherwise you will become a permorphous polyvert. There is no other word for it (bad luck).

According to Freud, all babies are permorphous polyverts; but Freud is wrong. As Foggmeister exclaims, " The Freudian theory of polyversive permorphosis is subject to revision : babies that are not *handled* too much or in any way unduly *fondled* in early childhood develop into *non-polyversive monomorphs*."

That ought to comfort you, even if your mother can't.

At any rate, it should warn you. Tell your nurses and your mothers and

Permorphous polyvert

your god-aunts that they are not to over-dandle you, or dangle you too much, or bungle you in any way. Let them trundle you a little or push you about gently with the soles of their feet, if they must ; but remember, *handling* is dangerous. . . .

Another thing—be careful how you allow people to approach you. If they approach you from behind when you are lying down, you will squint—and a perversive polymorph that squints is past analysis.

CHAPTER III

DANGER OF FIXATION

BE careful about the *first* things you do.

" Perverted primary actions " (as Fuggmeister incessantly shouts) " *lead inevitably to perverted secondary reactions which are immediately buried alive in the sub-conscious vital stream.*"

This just means that you become " fixated." In other words, if you want a drink the *first time* you feel thirsty you will find in later life that you will always feel thirsty whenever you want a drink.

You see the danger. You will get into bad habits. Eventually you will find that if you divorce your *first wife* you will always marry anyone you have divorced. . . .

Worse still : if you marry the *first girl* you fall in love with you will always fall into marriage with anyone you love. This is not only polymorphous, but illegal.

CHAPTER IV

CORRECT USE OF DREAMS

Do not imagine that, just because you are a Pre-adult, you are entitled to shirk having psymbolical dreams. Dreams are, of course, tremendously significant, and, *if dreamt properly*, and subsequently analysed properly, should at once reveal your normal hatred of your mother, or, better still, The Unfrustrated Intention to Eat The Grandfather (Bravo !).

If your dreams reveal nothing of the sort, then you are just *dreaming them wrong*. Go to sleep again at once ; and *have the dreams again until you get them right*.

Lots of people who, following Hoggmeister's rule, began life as babies in early youth, are now in Lunatic Asylums, Parliament, etc., simply through dreaming the wrong dreams. For instance, there are some (apparently normal in other respects) who often dream that they are at a football match with thousands of other people ! Others (quite business-like during the day) dream that they *are in the bath and cannot find the loofah*.

Beware ! The loofah-motif is unbelievably dangerous :—a certain well-known Monogamist who came to us for treatment was alarmed by having dreamt that he was *in a room with thousands of other loofahs* (but could not find the bath).

From this we were able to tell him that his wife had probably deserted him. . . . When M. went home, he looked for his wife in all the usual places and could not find her, and it subsequently turned out just as we had said ; she had properly deserted him—*taking the loofah withah !*

Or take the famous Débâcle case, of which most pre-adults have heard—but not the whole truth, which we reveal here for the last time :—Monsieur Débâcle was a china merchant in Rouen ; one night he woke up automatically at 3 a.m., *contrary to his usual custom*, having dreamt very vividly that there was a *Bull* in his shop.

On going downstairs he discovered that *it was a Cow*. . . .

We might add that as a result of this shock Monsieur

Débâcle became abnormally Bull-conscious and was for years afterwards addicted to dream-psychophany or shouting (usually about bulls) in his sleep. Indeed, he only retained his sanity by adopting a course of well-thought-out *gestures of compensation* such as attiring himself in the uniform of a Beef-Eater, and making bull's-eyes at all his customers.

CHAPTER V

PSYMBOLOGISM

THAT shows what comes of not dreaming your dreams right in the pre-adult stage. In order to make quite sure that you are dreaming them right, you will be well-advised to make an intensive pre-adult study of normal pre-adult Dream-Psymbologism.

The normal images of most frequent occurrence in the normal pre-adult dream are, as a rule, practically normal and can be briefly summarised :—

(a) *Imago pater-familiensis* (or Images signifying your Father) : Serpents—finnan haddocks—boating hats—zebras—zip-fasteners.

(b) *Imago grandis-materfamiliensis* (or Images stigmatising your Grandmother) : Tree-lupins— lumps—dwarf-elephants—giant latch-keys—internal combustion engines.

Thus if you have a persistent dream that a zebra wearing a boating hat is trying to insinuate lumps of finnan haddock into your dwarf-elephant's internal combustion engine you will realise that you are obsessed with your ancestry in the normal ratio of 2 : 2, that your absorption in the lower branches of the family tree is proportionally rational, and that you are in fact *quite all right.*

Quite all right

CHAPTER VI

SOME TYPICAL TYPES

WHEN you grow up you will become an Adult Only. But all adults are divided into Types: so consider carefully before it is too late which of these you want to be:

The types usually considered worth consideration are :—

(a) The commonly insane.
(b) The uncommonly stupid or Happy-go-Ugly Morons; including Motons (auto-erotics) which

(b)

care more for motor-cars than for people; and other variants, such as (i) Photons (or Moovi-morons) which will not read and cannot under-stand anything unless they see it in " pictures," and (ii) Photomatons, which continually take snapshots without realising what they have done.

(c) Freud's Preposterot or Polymorphous Phrenopod (with brains in feet, etc.), including subconscious ball-room dancers, and football addicts.

(d) The Thyroid or Apex Baboon of No Known Function.

The choice is in reality even more extensive ; but a word of warning. Do not attempt to confuse or con-

Somebody will notice it

ceal your Type. If you are subconsciously ugly, or subcutaneously stupid, sooner or later the fact will come to the surface : somebody will notice it.

None of these types are *perfect :* indeed, the perfectly balanced condition, in which the Psycho-vacuum (or soul) becomes Totally Equated (i.e. perfectly Aimless) is probably unattainable even by brand-new pre-adults. . . .

Probably
unattainable

But Buggmeister has summed all this up in the now universally accepted rule that

" *Something is Wrong with Everybody* " (bad luck)
(Buggmeister, passim)

From which Fuggmeister has deduced (he would) that

"*Everything is Wrong with Somebody* "
(Fuggmeister, cursim)

And sooner or later you will have to answer the utterly Freudful question—" Is it Me ? "
But not yet.

CONCLUSION

And now, sweet polymorph, it is high time, according to the Mothercraft Manual, for you to re-enter the land of Polymorpheus ; in short, you've got to go really and Truby to sleep and run over those psymbols once more to make sure you've got them right.

At the risk, therefore, of permanently blighting your psyche we will attempt to soothe you with a teeny-weeny psycho-lullabye, thus :

PSYCHO-LULLABYE

Hushabye Babies
(*Hush quite a lot*)—
Bad Babies get Rabies
(And have to be shot).
So suck the right fingers,
And dream the right dreams,
(*And don't you wake up with*
Psymbolical Pscreams !)

PSYMBOBLIOGRAPHY

A Jung Man's Fancy . .	by S. Freud
Who's a Freud? . . .	by A Jung Man
Cherchez la Gran'mère . .	by W. Foggmeister— Wild Professor of A-moral Philosophy, University of Tunbridge Wells
Things that Go Womp in the Night	by Prof. Angus McBoggart, University of Peebles

(And by the same author—

The Problem of the Peeble-Minded)

She-Stupes to Conquer .	by An Eminent Stupologist

Read also :—

A Mid-Summer Night's Dream and	
Symboline	by W. Shakespeare
Little Worrit . . .	
and	
The Wind in the Pillows .	by Walter Pater

IV

GEOGRAPHY PART I

ARCHIPELAGOES AND ALL THOSE

Absolutely Geographical Scene in Mungo Park (N. Laxative Isles) ; showing clearly, *Mungo Trees, Breadfruit palm, Fruit-bread bushes, Grape-fruit gums, Nut-cutlet groves* and belts and belts of *Exporto Grass*

I. THE SECRET

AFTER an unparalleled research we are now able to reveal the great Secret of Geography. The secret is that *without Geography you would be quite lost* : you wouldn't know where you were, or whether you were a native or British, or where the nearest mangrove swamp was, or anything ; you wouldn't even be sure whether you lived on an alluvial plain or not !

You wouldn't know

And there are other dangers : without Geography you might fail to recognise the signs of the Zodiac and it would be *on you like a flash !* Or you might plunge recklessly into the sea at Brighton without realising that *" the ridge connecting the Aleutian Islands with Kamschatka prevents the cold water from the bottom of the Bering Sea from entering the main body of the Ocean. . . ."*

II. UTTERLY PRACTICAL

Thus, as everybody agrees nowadays, Geography is the most *practical* thing in Education : most important of all, perhaps, it tells you *where things are*, so that if you want a Delta, or some Archipelagoes, or a Bunyan tree, or as much Exporto grass as possible, then by means of Geography you know at once where to go and get them.

Or suppose you found yourself stranded on an iceberg in the Arctic Zone. You could be absolutely certain that, owing to Geography, there was *far more of the iceberg under the water than was visible to the naked eye.*

Finally, if you didn't know Geography, *you could never circumnavigate the globe*, or build a watershed, or pass the simplest examination (in Geography).

In the last resort you might not even be able to *teach Geography !*

NOTE : If you are depressed about All This, and feel utterly ignorant, *see Relief Map* (fig. 1).

(Fig. 1)

III. HOW TO BEGIN

For the benefit of beginners it is customary to divide Geography into Mathematical Geography, Stratospherical Topography, Political Geology, Commercial Astronomy, and Marine Doxology.

Once you have begun, however, you will find it even more customary to forget these divisions, and a good deal more consoling to cast your eye rapidly over Figs. II, III and IV—*Useful Geographical Conceptions.*

Having absorbed *All These* you must be reminded that it is always considered sporting to examine, at this early stage, what is known as

IV. THE CONFORMATION OF THE GLOBE

The facts about this are simple enough : during the day the globe is always the right way up ; during the night it is, consequently, always upside down.

USEFUL GEOGRAPHICAL CONCEPTIONS

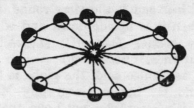

Fig. ii. The Equatorial Enigma

Fig. iii. Problem Performed by the Globular Anomaly

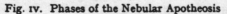

Fig. iv. Phases of the Nebular Apotheosis

Thus, if the globe were flat, everything would fall off it during the night (bad luck).

But it's *all right*. Owing to Geography, the globe *rotates on its axis* and is therefore round, so that you can't tell when it is upside down and when it isn't. Consequently *nothing falls off*. (*Touch wood. See Relief Map* at once, if necessary.)

(In short, as Galileo said, the globe is an Obsolete Spheroid, and, as Senior Geography Mistresses so wisely insist, it's Geography, not Love, that makes the world go round.)

Actually it is quite easy to *prove* that the globe is round. You can do this either

(i) By watching a ship sailing away into the distance : when it gets dark, you can't see the ship any longer.

or (ii) By noticing that, when you are at the seaside, you always see the tops of things first.

or (iii) By gazing for 360 degrees through a circular telescope until you see the back of your own head.

or (iv) By dropping yourself and a pebble simultaneously off the Leaning Tower of Pisa. (Galileo's experiment.)

(N.B. Either the pebble or you will reach Pisa first : the *editor's decision is futile*.)

V. POSITION OF THE GLOBE IN SPACE

Besides being round, itself (round itself, etc.), the globe has become implicated in a number of external rotatory movements (or perigoroundidtudes) without which the whole of Geography would immediately come to a standstill (or solstice).

These movements explain clearly the position of the globe in space and are themselves explicable, inexplicable, etc., by 3 possible systems (i) *The Stellar System*, which is far too decentralised to be memorable, (ii) *The Solar System*, which is far too concentric to be natural and (iii) *The Sellar System*, which though slightly eccentric is not only memorable but definitely consoling.

According to the latter system there are 3 main rotatory movements.

(*a*) The Sun (or Solar Globe) rotates round its own axis on an epileptic cycle every 365 years.

(*b*) The Earth (or Terrestrial Globule) rotates
    (i) round itself every 28 days—this movement was for centuries a mystery but is now explained by astronomers as being partially due to the *Rotation of the Earth*.
    (ii) round the Sun (or Solar Globe) once in a blue moon (i.e. 3·141592653589793233842916728324 1265 times per Lunar Month).

(*c*) The Moon (or Lunar Pillule) rotates round Something or other every now and then (or Grand Lunatic Year).

The only remaining question is " *What rotates round the Moon ?* " The answer is Nothing (bad luck—Woe is Moon).

VI. DAYS OF THE WEEK. GREGORIAN CALENDAR, ETC.

During the darkness and confusion of the Dark Ages it frequently happened that the *Calendar got lost* so that differences of opinion arose about the Days of the Week, Bank Holidays, etc., and there was serious danger of a general loss of faith in the inevitability

of Sunday. Pope Gregory, however, issued directions
(at the Council of Greenwich, 321 B.C.) that the Days
of the Week should always follow each other in the
same order, and arrangements were therefore made
that *the Earth should invariably rotate in the same
direction.*

This, however boring it may be to you personally, is
very safe, and right, and you know it.

For instance, if the Earth were to rotate from left
to right during the day and from right to left during the
night, to-day would only be yesterday over again,
while to-morrow, Saturday afternoon, etc., would never
come and race suicide on an enormous scale would
ensue. As things are, see Relief Map quickly and touch
wood again.

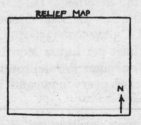

RELIEF MAP

N

VII. STRUCTURE OF THE EARTH—AGENTS

Originally the Globe was all spread out level at the
bottom of the sea. But early Geographers soon discovered that this geologically faultless arrangement
was a drag on the evolution of the British Empire ;
and so by a slow process of folding and crumbling and
squeezing from side to side enormous continents of
land, hope, glory, etc., began to appear.

So far, so good.

But the structure of the Earth cannot be dismissed entirely at this juncture (bad luck). In the interests of Geography, *various AGENTS are constantly at work* reducing the Earth's crust to small particles, carrying the crumbs from higher to lower levels, distributing the sand unfairly among the seaside resorts, and in extreme cases, *eating away the coast-line*.

It is absolutely essential *to get in well with these Agents*, since it is they who are responsible for all the absolutely *Geographical Things* found in the world, most of which are extraordinarily disagreeable, e.g. Waterspouts. Waterspats. Landslips. Sandbeds (especially at the seaside), Sandflips and Landslaps—not to mention all the innumerable eruptions, erosions and totally unconsoling geographical explosions, without which Geography would be reduced to at least one lesson a week, and might even cease to be General Knowledge altogether.

Stonehenge (by kind permission of the Dean)

VIII. GEOGRAPHICAL THINGS

We have thus arrived at the most important question in all Geography.

Which things are Geographical Things ?

Every right-thinking person will recognise at once that such things as Sponges, Tundras, Table-lands and Cameroons are exquisitely geographical, whereas Sponge-cakes, Tumblers, Table-napkins and Macaroons are not geographical at all.

But how, it may be asked, can one tell for certain, when confronted by any particular case ? There is no set rule. Ultimately it is a matter of cultured taste, of Geographical *flair* or flavour.

Generally speaking, however, anything thoroughly remote, romantic and utterly unremunerative that the Man in the Street is never likely to run across (in the Street), anything which blows you sky-high or lets you down thousands of feet, anything which is, whatever way you look at it, *peculiar*, and (*a*) easy to remember, like *archipelagoes*, or (*b*) difficult to remember, like *isotherms*, and absolutely anything ending in " -oon," is probably *Geographical* all right.

Thus, once again :

Geographical : Hailstorms, maelstroms, sandstorms, bandstorms, landsturms, a confluence, The Doldrums, exporto-grass, etc.

Non-Geographical : Bathing-beaches, bus-stops, toast, lawn-mowers, golf-courses, bear-gardens, beer-gardens, braces, etc.

Or, looking at the question from a slightly different, but equally Geographical angle, all the Things which are unquestionably *Imports and Exports* can safely be classed as profoundly Geographical.

Most of these are quite unmistakable, e.g.: *Sandwiches* (from the Sandwich Islands); *Thursdays* (from the Thursday Islands); *Men* (with hats), (from Manhattan); *Massage* (from Patagonia); *Lozenges* (from Los Angeles); *Bombs, Bits of Biscuits, etc.* (from The Bite of Bombiscay); and, of course, *Exporto Grass* (from Everywhere).

(N.B. For other consoling Imports and Exports see Conceivable Countries, pp. 59–80.)

The Royal Exchange, Liverpool : birthplace of Charlotte Brontë

IX. LINES

But the most exclusively Geographical Things of all are unquestionably the innumerable LINES with which the whole globe has become cat's-cradled owing to the continual and uncontrolled increase of Geography, and which all experts profess to consider *essential to true Geographical enjoyment*.

In ancient times the world was commendably free of all this distracting woof-work and, to be quite honest, our researches have failed to reveal even at the present day any *strong public demand* for these Geographical Lines—with two notable exceptions :

(i) The grand basic Line or Terrestrial Cummerbund known as the Equator, which is, as everyone admits, imaginary, invisible, invariable, but agreeably navigable and utterly memorable—in fact, generally speaking, a thoroughly good all-round Line.

(ii) The fine old hard and fast *Lines of Latitude and Longditude*, also *Uptitude*, *Wrongditude*, *etc.* Everyone seems agreed that Geography would never be quite the same again if these were rubbed out, and that, although of no commercial significance (*Mercator's Objection*), there is something soothing about the way they go up and down and to and fro and all meet at the North and South Poles ; and something rather touching about the deep pleasure they give to sailors, who, we understand, cling to the belief that they are all parallel.

On the whole, since they enable you to calculate how long a country is—longditude—and how far you can let yourself go—latitude—we are inclined to vote that it is well worth the expense of marking them out every year and that it is never too early, though usually too late, to commit these excellent Lines to memory.

Stalactites (by kind permission of the Stalagmites)

X. WHICH THINGS ARE WHICH

You will not deny that any day you might find your-self in the middle of a waterless desert surrounded by hordes of deadly veiled Arabs (or Cook's Touaregs); and that they would probably suspect a trap and put you to a good deal of expense, torture, etc., if you went up and asked the way to the nearest Archipelago . . . when what you really wanted was an Oasis.

It is therefore not only necessary to know all the Geographical Things by heart but also to know *Which Things are Which*.

Fortunately a certain number of them, such as isotherms, isthmuses, etc., can be disthmissed with a brief definition, e.g. :

An Isthmus.   A bit of land that juts into two other
              bits of land.

A Strait.	A bit of sea that juts out of two other bits of sea.
An Island.	A little bit of land jutting out of a previous Age, with no visible means of support.
Archipelagoes.	Enormous extinct Arctic birds that jut their fossil eggs into the mouths of extinct volcanoes.
Glaciers.	Huge rivers of ice that come rushing down from the mountain-tops at the rate of two inches a year and engulf whole villages during the night.
Hemi-sphere (or Demi-monde)	Any one half of the earth which has been led astray from any other half or for any other reason has got jutted on to the opposite page of the Atlas.
Isotherm.	(Deriv. Gk. *Isos*, cold. *Thermos*, a flask.) Hot and Cold Line connecting people of the same mean annual temperatures with equally mean people having the same annual colds, flasks, thermometers, etc.

As for the rest, readers who still find themselves in any kind of doubt as to *which Things are Geographical* or *Which Things are Which* should, before attempting the study of Conceivable Countries (p. 59), take one final glance at the Relief Map and then plunge without further delay into the SARGASSO SEA in order to conduct a personal Research there.

This indispensable middle-water or vortical muddle-centre of the Earth will be found to contain *Everything which has been left over from the rest of Geography,* including Sampans, Rickshaws, Aqueducts, The Gulf Stream, Stalagmites, Dologmites, Marsupials, The Purile Islands, and, need we add ?—*hitherto undreamt-of* quantities of *Exporto Grass.*

XI. PROPOSAL FOR A GEOGRAPHICAL HOLIDAY

We hope we have now made it abundantly clear that there are *far too many Geographical Things.* If you have the slightest doubt about that, perhaps you would like to stay in next Saturday afternoon while we tell you (in addition to All This) All You Know about Deltas, Estuaries, Lines of No Variation, Belts of No Vegetation and the innumerable Torrid, Currid, Marrid (and collectively Horrid) ZONES with which this Pestilestial Globe is hachured.

If you would rather not be worrid any more, you had better support our utterly consoling geo-surgical proposal for *A Perpetual Geographical Holiday ;* for the purpose of which a selected part of the World Map will, by a Decree Nihil, be declared a *Zone of No Geography* or total Geo-Nography.

In this area we should of course decapitate all the headlands, unbutton the capes, damn the rivers, dismantle the water-sheds, make molehills out of the Mts., prohibit all Imports and Exports (we are glad to note that most countries have practically done this already) and make it a capital offence even to mention Exporto Grass.

In this way and in this way only shall we prevent Geography gradually becoming the Top, or even the only, Subject in Education and postpone indefinitely

the Apotheosis of the Geography Master (and Mistress)
—the which would be a Bad Thing, believe us.

TEST PAPER
ON
GEOGRAPHY PART I

1. " East is East and West is West." *Show, by shading, if this is a fact or only a brilliant conjecture.*
   Criticise your answer in the light of the Midnight Sun.

2. Mt. Everest is 29,002 ft. high. Do you consider this sufficient ?

3. At noon on the 21st of October *show, by shading the eyes, how high the sun will be above the horizon*
   (*a*) At the Horizon,
   (*b*) At noon on the 21st of October.

4. You are required to indicate by a dot the 50 Largest Towns and also the 4 Longest Rivers in N. America. *Where would you put the dot?*

5. (i) Would you mind putting your finger on
   (a) An Archipelago; (b) A Volcano; (c) A Cactus Plant.

   (ii) Would you mind not drawing things on the Blotting-paper?

6. Explain in round terms your opinion of
   (a) The Equator
   (b) The problem performed by the Globular Anomaly.
   (c) Tapioca.

7. Draw a map of a Place and write (or draw) coal, tin, woollens, muffins, cushions, tapioca, etc., all over the Place.

8. The Annual Rainfall of the Isle of Mull is 100 *inches continuous.* Are you prepared to sit down under this?

9. "From the Sago palm, 10 days' labour will obtain sufficient sago to last a man for a year." But what use would the man be next year?

10. What makes you think (a) that the Panama Canal is a kind of connecticut joining N. and S. America? (b) that the capital of America is New York and (c) that Immigrants turn back on seeing the gigantic Statue of Prohibition erected by President Thingammy Hall?

11. If a line were drawn between Warsaw and Yokohama, would you be in favour of War with Japan?

V

PRACTICE AND FURY OF KNITTING

PART I. THEORETICAL

NOTE : *Readers of this important Section of The Hole Pocket Treasury who are old enough to be confirmed Woologists, i.e. those who are definitely committed to Knitting for life, will perhaps prefer to pass on at once to Part II, which is devoted to everything you know already about Practical Knitcraft.*

Part I is recommended especially to Woological agnostics, who will find the tremendous question, ' Is Knitting Justifiable ? ' thoroughly thrashed out here for the first time.

CHAPTER I

CAUSE OF KNITTING

ALTHOUGH not as yet scheduled by the Board of Trade as a fatal occupation, Knitting is now recognised to be by no means so harmless, or so innocent a way of behaving as our ancestors apparently believed it to be.

The uncontrollable impulse which comes to all women, sooner or later, to knit Something, however melancholy, and even to wear it afterwards, is due basically to a *craving for excitement*—to the human but unhealthy desire to mystify oneself and other people, and to perform *aggressive and risky actions.*

However
melancholy

BARBED WIVES

This was brought out most clearly in the earlier part of the Great War, when it was noticed that while the soldiers unostentatiously occupied their evenings with the simplest forms of woven wire-work, the women and children of all nations fell into frenzies of belligerent and dangerously speculative Knitting. (See fig. i, *Mouffler en Surprise.*)

Fig. i
Mouffler en Surprise

CHAPTER II

HOW DANGEROUS IS IT ?

AFTER a long and unreknitting investigation of the statistics of Knitting fatalities we are happy to record that the Knitting Toll is diminishing. Woological accidents of several kinds continue, however, to recur: they are due usually to

(i) *foul knitting*, i.e. unscrupulously raising the kneedles above the shoulders when attempting a particularly strong and decisive stroke.

(ii) *congested-knitting* (or " *slum-knitting* "), i.e. attempts by two or more cocoon-addicts to knit the same sock at the same time in some confined space such as a public telephone box or light aeroplane.

(iii) *Purlers*, i.e. serious knitfalls due to knitting inattentively in the hunting-field, or while running downstairs carelessly in the night-gown (or, more rarely, the wedding-dress).

THE HAMPSTEAD HEATH TRAGEDY

The most famous Knitting Tragedy of recent times (" *The Hampstead Tangle* ") was, however, of an even more intricate nature. We will recall the facts, since they are generally known to everybody.

A certain Mrs. C. was suddenly observed (by strollers on The Heath) to be fatally *intricated* with a well-dressed man wearing a thick astrakan coat. All attempts to extricate them proved unavailing and the two victims perished almost immediately. Believed at first to be the result of a suicide pact, the mystery was eventually unravelled with the aid of witnesses who testified to the fact that Mrs. C. was an *amazingly rapid knitter* and had already lost a dearly-loved sheep-dog under somewhat similar circumstances. The identity of the male victim was never established as he had been knitted out of all recogknition.

Such cases are, however, much less common than they used to be and the Modern Girl need have little anxiety about leaving her parents at home Knitting, in the Knitting-room, provided this is fairly spacious and the old people are of equable temperament. If these conditions are absent, it is, of course, best to leave them just Sitting, kneedless to say, in the Sitting-room.

We have only one more word of warning to mutter : if you are addicted to *Knitting while Eating* you should exercise some caution never to Eat what you are Knitting, or Knit what you are Eating, especially in the event of macaroni.

CHAPTER III

IS IT CREWEL ?

THERE are two common methods of Knitting which have often been stigmatised by soft-hearted people as *brutal;* namely, (*a*) Speculative Knitting, and (*b*) Knitting on the Model.

Speculative Knitting—performed *in vacuo* under the impression or delusion that if you go on Knitting long

Fig: 11. *Gent's Sleeveless Errand*
[N.B. *Every square, an inch : every inch, a gentleman*]

enough, with long enough Kneedles, Wool, etc., some form of Pilch-knicker or Squelch-bocker (suitable for a Baby or Infantryman) will ultimately occur—is in our opinion unfortunate rather than unkind (see fig. ii, *Gent's Sleeveless Errand*). The question of cruelty only arises when ruthless attempts are made to force the speculative Knit-work on to defenceless persons.

Knitting on the Model entails finding a willing Baby, or Officer, or Other Rank, surrounding it with kneedles and then completing the Knit-craft with unthinkable rapidity before the model grows up, retreats, or in some other way completely alters its shape or position.

It is interesting, by the way, to note that the International Speed Record for Deliberate Knitting on the Model is held by Fräulein Nähnadel of Prague, who circumknitted a 6-foot infantry sergeant in a field-green multiple belliclover, encompassed on 24 Kneedles, in 56 mins. 23 secs. (*Prosit !*)

But to return to our mittens ; knitting of these kinds is not, in our judgment, cruel. In the judgment of other experts it is *not even crewel*.

Knitting enthusiasts may therefore safely ignore all panicky attempts to brand Knitting as a bloodsport.

CHAPTER IV

SUMMARY : WHY KNIT ?

WHY Knot ?

PART II. PRACTICAL

The science of Knitting has been built up on two primary strokes, the Purl (abbr. P.) and the Plain (abbr. P.), which the following diagrams (1 and 2) make sufficiently P. (or P.).

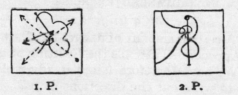

1. P.   2. P.

Other abbreviations to be found in all practical Knitting Recipes are K. 1 (Knit 1 stitch), U.K. 1 (Unknit 1 stitch), Ch. (Chain stitch), S.K. (Start Knitting, or Stop Knitting), G.K. (Go on Knitting), W.K. ! (Well-Knit !), D. ! (Damknit !), etc.

Any simple exercise will illustrate the use of these; e.g. :

TO KNIT (K) A GENT'S WHITE ENDLESS COMFORTER

S.K. K. 1. U.K. 1. P. 100. P. 200. D. ! K. 2 tog. P. 2000. (W.K. !) S.K. G.K. P. to K. 4. Kt. to

B. 3. B. to B. 4. Ch. D. ! (Both castle on.) B. takes P. P. takes Q. D. ! D. ! (Both castle off.) K. takes K. White to mate in 3 moves.

(N.B. If mate objects, huff him.)

White Endless Comforter

ADVANCED EXERCISE
To knit a ten-foot sock

N.B. A certain amount of danger (see Part I, Chap. II, also Appendix A) attends the Knitting of advanced socks. We have therefore found it advisable in this instance to write out the directions *in full*.

   1. Start Knitting.
   2. Knit 2 and 2 together.
   3. Drop one—there are now 3 left, therefore—
   4. Slip one, slop one, Knit to and fro.
   5. Heel and Toe.   1, 2, 3 Hop
                      Before and behind Hop
                      Weel may the keel row.

   6. Knit one, not two,
      Forget one, Knot two,
      Pick up one. Drop it. Undrop it.
      Damknit. Wherethehellisit ?

7. *To turn the heel*—
   Cast off 2 plain ;
   Cast them on again ;
   Now is the critical moment. Look carefully about you :
   It's no good casting off purl before swine.
   If all is well, cast off one purl.
   Look again ;
   Cast off purl rapidly·in all directions.
8. Breathe again.
9. After this, it's all plain Knitting, therefore—
   Drip one, drop one, Drop the sock—
   The sock is now grey, therefore—
   Continue Knitting grey socks for 18 more rounds.*
10. Finish off with buttons at toe and heel, and button-holes to correspond (if possible).

N.B. There should be holes at the top or elsewhere for inserting ribbons, feet, etc. If there aren't, it is not a sock at all, but a ten-foot cold comforter (bad luck).

For further examples, both simple and advanced, see figs. iii–ix, pp. 57–58.

APPENDIX A

Effect of Knitting on the Mind

ALTHOUGH Madness is, in our opinion, only rarely caused by Knitting, it is perhaps significant that the longest piece of unbroken solo knitting on record was at once the cause and the consequence of Mental Instability.

---

* If, after all these, the Knitter finds that he himself is becoming teased, twilled, tousled, and in fact practically worsted, he should, if a Christian, turn the other heel and Knit on Knotwithstanding.

This was a pinkish tubular tricotage begun, after much nervous hesitation, in December 1865 by a Bosnian Inspector of Police, name of Rosenpantz, who had for years nursed a devouring ambition to *Knit a pink sock.*

In February of the following year, finding himself unable to visualise the method of turning the heel, R. attempted to postpone the decision by changing his intention to that of *Knitting a pink stocking.*

The case first came to the notice of the Public in 1867 when R., having failed again and again, offered the piece, then some 3·64 metres in length, to the

Tiergartendirektor (lit. Zooheadkeeper) as a soft collar for Wintergiraffen.

On learning, however, that in the opinion of the Tiergartendirektor he was a Knitwit, R. definitely lost all mental stability and abandoned himself utterly, for 19 years, to an unbroken spell of Woological frenzy.

Following a shock in 1886, R. completely recovered his sanity. But realised that, though he could now turn the heel, the sock would never be any use owing to its extreme length (a little over 1008619392476·67 metres); and died, on July 9th, 1889, a sane but discomfortered man.

NOTE : The unfinished sock was, for years, one of the most treasured exhibits of the Museum of Unconsciously Psychological Crafts at Vienna, where it occupied a great deal of valuable space until the year 1918, when, following on the defeat of the Central Powers, it was divided equally among the Allies by the Treaty of Versailles.

APPENDIX B

Historical, Geographical, Statistical, etc.

¶ KNITTING starts mainly in Australia, where it is found in *the raw state* on the great Australian Bush. Here, when sufficiently ripe, it is harvested by the

indefatigable Bushwhackers. Thereafter it is dealt with direct on the famous Australian sock-rearing farms ; or else shipped to England, where by a complicated process of twisting and twining (and in obstinate cases twirling and twiddling) it is kneaded into long plaited buns or *chignons de laine* at Knottingham, or carded on to little pieces of card-board at Cardigan. It is by this time fully domesticated and ready to be unplaited again laboriously by hand (for some reason), rolled up into a ball (to amuse the cat), and finally entangled with the kneedles, legs of chairs, etc.

¶ The secret practice of knitting live Angora rabbits into muffs was forbidden by The Sublime Porte in 1761.

¶ In 1886 a project for a World Knitting Congress or Mammoth Woolgathering to be held in the old Winter Palace at Balaclava was put forward by the Lord Chancellor and Lady Mary Wolstencraft. It is calculated that the congress, if it had taken place, would have produced more than 12 million miles of Knitted matter. The project was abandoned owing to the opposition of the R.S.P.C.C., The Lord's Day Observance Society and other bodies devoted to Infant Welfare. Community Knitting is unlikely to raise its head again.

BIBLIOGRAPHY OF KNITTING

Knitting through the Ages . by Purl Lady Knott-
      ingham

A Stitch in Time . . . by Prof. A. Einstein

Lamb's Tanglewood Tails .

Life of Sir Garment Wolsey . by Lady Lindsey

Schnellnittungsbeginnungs (An
  Introduction to Speed
  Knitting) . . . by Fr. Nähnadel (of
      Prague)

    Read also, if possible :

Drip one Drop one (Verse) . by Woolhelmina Stitch

SIMPLE PRACTICAL EXERCISES FOR BEGINNERS

Fig. iii.   Dust Sheet for
Ham Sandwich

Fig. iv.   Body-belt for
Cobra

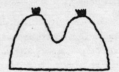

Fig. v.   Pull-over for
Dromedary

Fig. vi.   Pass-over for
Rabbi

Fig. vii.   Shawl-Coatee
for Winter Turnip

FUTILITY GARMENTS FOR ADVANCED KNITTERS

Fig. viii.   Cow-Cosy or
Milchcardigan (proceed
as for Child's Pilch-
breechette)

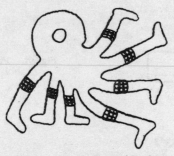

Fig. ix.   Golf Ensemble for
Octopus (or, Bag-pipe Cosy)

VI

GEOGRAPHY PART II

CONCEIVABLE COUNTRIES

SOMEHOW or other a large number of COUNTRIES have managed to worm their way into or in between the Geographical Things mentioned in Geography, Part I. Very few of them, however, are Absolutely General Knowledge.

We shall describe, therefore, only the more Conceivable sort of Countries—omitting Latvia, and Lithuania (not to mention Ireland, Poland, Germany and many others), as being *insufficiently typical of countries in general*, or, in some instances, *of themselves*, or alternatively as being *only too typical, topical, tropical, inconsolable, or even bogus* . . .

We are left with the following characteristic, conceivable and decently geographical countries.

CHAPTER I

EUROPE

NOTE : Throughout this section the natural spelling has been adopted for all place-names, ignoring merely local or native variations, e.g. Rome, not *Roma* ; Florence, not *Furore* ; Russia, not ⴄ∩SSI∀·

FRANCE

Principal Imports. *La Gloire, les Pourboires.*
Principal Exports. *Les Belles Lettres, Les Beaux Gestes, Les Bonjours et les Babas au Rhum.*

Principal Exceptions.   *Bijoux, cailloux, choux, genoux, hiboux, joujoux, poux.*

SECTION A.   PANORAMA GÉNÉRALE

(Very difficult ; dictionaries may be used)

La Belle France! One sees it all ; the panorama of the land. . . . First there is *M. le porteur* (65 Fcs.—woe is you) ; and then *M. le douanier* (everything to declare—woe is everybody) ; one takes the *auto-taxi* (woa is impossible, *M. le chauffeur* is full of *élan Vittel*) ; one voyages by the *chemin-de-fer,—avec les petites trompettes et les toot-toot-toot-la nuit.*

One apperceives also, undoubtedly, le Dellymell, le Smellysmell, and in the South, the beautiful *Midi*, one does *not* perceive the beautiful Race of the *Midinettes* (*hélas*).

Avez-vous vu la Tour Eiffel, grande tour de force parisienne? You recognised it at once? Bravo! *Avez-vous vu les plumes de ma tante, grand tour de chapeau anglais?* You have? Bad luck. *Alors, prenons un drinking, un apéritif* (whatever that is—not quite what you thought, however), *un whisky-gin*, by example, here in the *café*, in the *Avenue Maréchal Flaubert le XII*, or the *Boulevard Louis-mil-neuf-cent-quatre-vingt-quatorze*, or again the *Rue Honoré de Barsac* . . .

SECTION B.   PHYSICAL FEATURES, ETC.

Political Divisions

The country of France, although famous chiefly for its Exceptions (see above) such as jewels, pebbles, cabbages, knees, owls, playthings, and, of course, l***, is also remarkable in being divided into *Compartments*

(*Hommes* 40–*Chevaux* 8) administered by Prefects and Sub-prefects all of whom have passed their French examinations and been awarded their *baccalauréats*, *baccarats* and *highcockalauréats*.

Mountains

There are also in France some noticeable *Mountainous Features* including the *Massif Centrale* (see fig. i), the

Fig. i.
Massif Centrale

Fig. ii.
Puy de Dome

Mont de Piété, and the *Puy de Dome* (see fig. ii), not to mention the numerous smaller excrescences such as *plateaux*, *gateaux* and *chateaux*, especially on the river Loire.

Rivers

These include the *Rhône*, *Beaûne* and *Saône ;* and there may be others but they are not Generally *Naône*, with the exception of the Seîne at Paris, memorable for its splendid Bridges, the most famous being the *Pont Neuf*, though the others, e.g. the *Pont-et-un*, *Pont-deux*, *Pont-trois*, *Pont-quatre*, etc., are worth enumerating occasionally.

Costume

A very prominent feature in France and all of the most *high-life*, e.g. le *smoking*, *les golfings*, un *boating*, and the sky-blue uniforms or *overcôtes d'azur*. But above all, the hats of the men which are undoubtedly *très chic* but (*hélas*) *trop small*, even the highlife *Cap d'Antibes* and the charming *Casquette Crickette* (*casquette des sportmans* 18 *Fcs.*).·

Sports

Besides French Cricket (*at Lourdes*), there are *le cyclisme*, *le tourisme*, *le footing*, *le dancing*, *Heid and Sieck*, etc., all of which can be done without a dictionary. But the most famous sport is

THE SIGHTS OF PARIS

The first thing one sees in Paris is of course the beach, the magnificent *Paris Plage* whither resort all the notables, such as the famous gastronome Count Louis de Bortsch, the fascinating Mlle le Bagage, and the sinister Don Juan les Pins. After that one usually visits the famous picture galleries such as the *Galeries Lafayette*, and the galleries of the *L'Ouvre* (usually shut) ; or the *Arc de Triomphe* (commemorating Joan of Arc) ; or the exhibitions of instruments of torture (*Tuileries*), in the great *Palais de Danse* at *Versailles*. But the most famous sight of all is the *Sight of the Pastille*, which is no longer visible : there is, however, a tablet there (unveiled recently by President Lozenge).

NOTE : *This frightful symbol of Affliction was the cause of the French Revolution because the Sight of the Pastille so enraged the mob that they started the French Revolution (thus destroying the Pastille).*

Fauna

France contains a number of very interesting animals, e.g. the irritating little *bêtes-noires*, and the *chamois* (charming little yellow animals made of leather). Edible animals include frogs, snails and puppy dogs' tails, the disappointing fishes called *poissons d'avril*, and, among birds, the elusive *Mallarde Imaginaire* (Eng. Bombay duck).

BELGIUM (OR NETHERLAND)

Belgium is memorable (" Remember Belgium ! ") principally as the place where the English have fought all their foreign wars since 1066 (when foreign wars in England were forbidden) and in consequence is referred to historically as the Cockshy, or Shostolpit, of Europe.

Not a geographical country in the true sense : contains no geysers, volcanoes or exports grass, and consists mainly of *undulating Uplands* in the North, *upulating Downlands* in the South, and numerous silly little lakes and streams (Flem. *Zillebekes*) which overflow themselves, especially in winter, thereby turning the whole country into one vast *Mudflat* or *Fludmap*, especially all the year round.

Population (comprising Belgian-speaking Belgians in the North and a few woollen-speaking Woollens in the South) is the densest in the world (bad luck). Education, however, compulsory.

Chief Manufactures

Linen and woollen and silken and woollen and pilkhem, and flaxen and other *Steinwerk*.

HOLLAND (or NOTHERLAND)

Holland is the lowest of the Low Countries and enjoys very poor physical features : it is, in fact, a low-lying country full of low, lying people whose main object in life is to *deceive the English* by holding *Dutch Auctions*, displaying *Dutch Courage* and talking *Double-Dutch*, etc.

To prevent themselves feeling low, the Dutch have planted their landscapes with Windmills, Belfries, Black Tulips and other Bulbous things—and, in addition to these Exterior characteristics they are notable for their indefatigable Dutch Interiors which enable them to thrive on nothing but cyder (Dutch : zuyder) and cheese (D. : tjeez).

Culture, Language, etc.

Culture, of course, like everything else, is at a low level and the people (it is one of their worst physical features) are, naturally, low-brows. They speak, ordinarily, Low Dutch, a language consisting of improper names (such as Amsterd**, and R********, etc.), and English speldt wrong (see examples above). For instance, when you hear a man in Holland say to another man, " Hoek it ! " or " Bergen-Op-Zoom ! " you know at once that he is angry, or zumpthing.

Strategic Idea

Holland (as hinted, possibly, above) is below sea-level (D. : zee-lüffel) ; in time of war, therefore, when the Dutch of course feel too low-spirited to put up a fight, they just inundate the Hole of Holland (or

Central Depression) by Sluyding the Sluice-gates at Flushing, or, alternatively, by Flooding the Flushgates at Sluys.

General Conclusion

Holland is just a low-down place, anyway.

SWITZERLAND

Configuration

Switzerland is an utterly perpendicular or funicular kind of country, consisting of innumerable soft white mountains such as Mont Blange, Blont Mange and The Alps, and an equal number of bottomless Pitz and Valais : if smoothed out flat it would take up a great deal of room ; but, as it is, it is quite small and is divided into (i) The famous climbing and ski-ing district known (for Shorts) as The Bareknese Oberland and (ii) The famous ski-ing and climbing district gloomily referred to by the Swiss as The English Ingedean.

Switzerland is also conscientiously divided into Compartments or Bitzerland, called Cantons, such as *The Grisons, Grimpons, Crampons, Simplons* and *Simpletons ;* but nobody seems to care about them much.

Towns (or Thuns)

Few but famous and found in confused groups or *klosters* on the banks of equally confused lakes, e.g. *Lusanne, Laucerne, Logano* and *Lucarno ;* the most

geographical town is Geneva, which is the Seat of the
League of Nations and thus known as The Home of
Lost Clauses ; it also is on a lake but is distinguishable
at once by the gigantic Protocol or secret palace built
(by Santa Clause) for the League of Nations to make
treaties against each other in.

Language

None. On parle français. Mann spricht Deutsch.
Englishspok (Donmenschnit).

Sports

None.

Industries

Ski-ing, Climbing, Cocktails (2/6), Lemon Squash
(1/6), Skating, Ski-joring, Tea (3/-), Gala Nights
(extra), and various forms of Ragging, Tagging and
Bobtailing.

Natives

Practically none : no room for them owing to surfeit
of industries (see above).

Reported to be sturdy and expert with the cross-
bow, and at their best playing a lugeing game. Not
much is generally known about the Swiss as they are
mostly compelled to shilly-shally in chilly châlets, or
perhaps bahns, during summer, winter, etc., to prevent
their getting in the way of the English, Germans and
other *Inhabitants*. The native costume is suspected

to consist of Shirtz, Shortz, Alpen-hatz, Rucksokz and Alpen-bootz.

Vice among the Natives

Practically none. Some Yodelweiss and a good deal of charging for the bath (Heisses-Wasserweiss).

Manufactures

Milk, Chocolate, Milk-Chocolate, Chocolate-Milk, fretwork Alpen-clocks, woodwork Bears and won'twork Watches.

Government

Switzerland is ruled by the Alpine and Ski Clubs of the various races of Inhabitants and operated by Guides and Kurvereins which provide snow, ice, curves, etc. as required, and maintain all glaciers, crevasses and avalanches in working order.

Current Coin

English cheques, Swiss francs, German marks, Norwegian telemarks.

National Anthem

Funiculi-funicular !

Days of the Week

Lunnday, Murrenday, Lugesday, Wengensday, Thawday, Freidegg and Scheidegg.

ITALY

Configuration, etc.

Italy is above all things fortunate in its shape which is *the only Natural Joke in Geography*. As against this, however, it is only fair to add that " *in the North, The Alps* " (contrary to their usual custom) " *descend with unusual abruptness into the plains of Lombardy* " : this is no joke and is probably very dangerous for Sombardy.

Rivers and Lakes

There are a number of beautiful *lakes* worth mentioning, including Lakes Maggiore, Minore and Plentimore. The only *potently memorable* Italian *river*, however, is *patently unmentionable :* the rivers of Italy are, therefore, in practice, seldom mentioned (bad luck).

Seats

Italy is famous for its Ancient Seats, e.g. Parma and Modena and Salteena, seats of Ancient Dukes, Granddukes and Great-grand-dukes (mostly dead now) ; and Sienna, seat of Ancient Art Critics (all burnt now) ; and the memorable Papal Seats or Veteran Palaces of The Popes at Rome, such as The Lutheran, The Vertical and The Esquilateral.

History

Italy has an enormous amount of mediæval history, most of it concentrated at *Venice*—at that period a great banking centre and governed by Doges of a rich nature (riotous old men who instituted the memorable

Venetian Blinds and originated the riotous Italian method of singing technically known as *blotto voce*.

NOTE : Formerly the Financial Whirlpool of the World, Venice is now the Blackpool of Italy, where British lovers steal about conscientiously in water-taxis (Ital. *Giocondolas*), in search of past Romance, future memories, and, in extreme cases, the Leaning Tower of Pisa.

Blotto voce

Government

Monarchy with Dictator, Shirts, etc.

Chief Inhabitants

(1) *H.H. The Pope of Rome*, who is immobile.
(2) *The Woman* (Ital. : *La Donna*), who, as everyone knows, is mobile.

Sports, etc.

Tempted by the coloured shirts (red, black, magenta and solferino) which are a dominant feature of the country the Italians have made notable attempts to play games, but are handicapped by a tendency to burst into song at cover point, in the goal mouth, etc. Sport has therefore been practically abandoned except for the giant Carnera marbles; though foreigners are still permitted to play Lido, Marco Polo, etc., at Brioni.

Chief Exports

Formerly; Roman Eagles, Ut (with the Subjunctive), Papal Bulls and other indulgences. Now; High-power Tenors (*lotta-voce*), Macaronigrams, and eponymous shirts.

Chief Imports

Formerly; Hannibal, Vegetebal, Minneral, etc. Now; Honeymoons (Ital. : *fondagondola*) : and Highbrows (*fonda-Croce*).

SPAIN AND PORTUGAL

NOTE : Portugal can be dismissed at once. (See Relief Map.)

SPAIN

Owing probably to the sunny good-nature of its geographical Dons, Spain has always been the most

geographically consoling country in the world, being practically square in shape and offering unrivalled amenities in the form of table-lands, water-partings and especially the extensive Series (Span. : *Sierras*) of

Sierras (Eng. : Mountains), all of which are parallel, horizontal, confluent and thus entirely consoling. What is even more gratifying, Madrid was deliberately chosen (by Charles V) as the capital city on the ground that it was *plumb in the middle !*—a reason which, we venture to say, would not have been considered valid (Sp. : *valadolid*) in any other country.

Inhabitants, Industries, etc.

Coming of a proud, sombre and somewhat cynical stock (especially the Undelusians of the South) the Spaniard is always a perfect gentleman, professing usually to be occupied in one of the old Spanish Crafts and to be proud of his skill as a Robber (Sp. : *Picador*), or Postman (*Ratatatador*) or Lorry-driver (*Lorreador dos Autos da Fé*) or Pullman attendant (*Correador*). The truth however is that they are all engaged in the *Mañana* Industry—carried on preferably in comfortable sunny places, such as parks and open-air cafés (Sp. : *Outadors*).

Chief Industry

National Sports

Formerly : Bull-fights, Basque-fights, Basquinadoes, Tilting at Windmills, and Old Spanish Dances (Sierras of Girdlequivers).

Now : Futbol, Pelota (or Basquetbol), Mañana, and (in Majorca) Singing in the Train (tunes : " Toreador-Tum-Tumti-Tumti-tum " ; " O Dear, What can the Matador," etc.).

N.B. Private Spitoons meet all trains free of charge and are provided *gratis* in 1st class Railway carriages.

Exports

The Spanish are too proud to export anything, but permit the English to come and fetch sherry as required.

Imports

Rain, Borrowed Bibles, and anything else permitted by the Old Spanish Customs.

Government

Republic with Dictators (Portugal : Dictator with Republics).

National Diet

Sherry, Oranges, Onions and Cascara Sagrada Mañana.

MUDDEL EUROPA

Before the Great War this medium-sized Geographical nuisance, variously referred to as the Mittle Entente, The Balkans, or Littel Europa, was the cause of a good deal of rather breathless *diplomatic duplicity*

such as AustriaHungary, BosnianHerzegovina, Mol-
davianWallachia and other *Double Ententes*.

But owing to a widespread feeling after the War
that what Muddel Europa wanted was more Geography
and less History, the inhabitants were compelled to
forgo their massachistic policy of being massocred
whenever possible by The Ottoman Turk and get on
with their agriculture, i.e. the cultivation of Oats,
Goats and Croats on the Adriatic sea-board, and their
commerce, e.g. the export of waltzes from Vienna,
rhapsodies from Hungary, spotted dog from Dalmatia,
czocholates from Czocholoslovakia and Funding Debts,
Sinking Bonds and Dud Czechs from everywhere.

British attitude to All This :—*Britons never (never)
shall be Slavs.*

CHAPTER II

THE COMMONWEALTH OF ETCETERAS

THE apotheosis of this part of Geography is, we need
hardly say, the British Commonwealth of Independent
Self-contained, Self-defensive Etceteras, consisting
mostly of Dominions—so called, probably, because
they have dominion over palm and pine and Us—and
at one time insultingly referred to as The British Empire
(bad luck, bad manners, etc.).

*Configuration. Inhabitants. Configuration of Inhabi-
tants, etc.*

The vast open spaces of the Dominions are thinly
populated (or according to some authorities sparsely
inhabited) by hardy races of vast thin he men and
sparse spacious she-women, who live splendidly

geographical lives of hardship and sparseship in the vast
densely-scattered overgrowth and the even vaster thin
parsley-matted under-scrub. As a result, these splendid
Domineers are better than the English at everything
(e.g. cricket, football, shooting, natives, shooting
natives and above all Roughing It)—except a few
things which don't matter, vastly (such as poetry,
dentistry, modesty, trousers, top-hats and following the
blue lights for Tooting station).

Roughing It, of course, means that you have to *do
everything for yourself :* for instance, a Man in a Dominion would have to grow his own clothes, blow his own
nose (trumpet, etc.) and so on, until he was hard enough
and vast enough and scrubby enough to admit that he
had beaten about enough Bush and was ready to stop
Roughing It in a rickshack at Timbuctoo and retire home
and try gruffing it in a bath-chair at Tunbridge Wells.

Some Typical Dominions

It would be difficult (and probably very dangerous) to
attempt to differentiate between the various Dominions

in the matter of Hardships, Vastness, Sparseships, Parsnips and other insignia of Independence.

But no Australian, for instance, need bother to deny that *CANADA* is completely made up of snow, so that everyone is compelled to mush about with mush-quash rackets tied to the soles of their feet ; and that the inhabitants, *habitants*, etc., are mostly great lumber-ing chaps who spend their time log-rolling in lumber-rooms with their untameable house-wives or huskies ; and that the chief exports are the furs of rare wild animals such as the beaverised lamb coney, the broad-tailed nutria, the lynx, the mynx (or manx lynx) and of course the ubiquitous mushquash.

As for *AUSTRALIA*, no Canadian need bother to forget that the Australians are Marsupials (in the case of the men, Parsupials) and that Australia suffers from Bad Luck all round, the Geography books agreeing that " its coasts are *uninteresting* and for the most part *without inlets* " (bad luck) ; and that there are " vast tracts in the interior that are doomed for ever to remain *without inhabitants* " (bad luck again), and " *alligators in all the rivers* " (bad management). . . .

At the same time no one will deny that life in Australia is so Rough that it is just heart-breaking and horse-breaking and soul-searing and sheep-shearing —in fact, utterly marsupial—and that Australia imports *Ashes* quite easily from England, and exports *Raw Knitting* and goes to war in the same kind of hat as *NEW ZEALAND ;* which has far better luck* and is suspected of being altogether *not so tough* (though it exports tons of frozen mutton), and which

* Except for the melancholy Kiwi bird which " is *not a mar-supial* " (bad luck) and has " only *rudimentary wings* and *no tail* " (Can you beat it ?).

has a *Native question*, which used to be so Aukward because the Natives (Maoris, etc.) were almost as splendid as the New Zealanders (Laoris, etc.) so that the only thing to do was to tell them both to get as brown as possible and call them All Blacks, and pack them down 2 : 3 : 2 with three three-quarters and two five-eighths and watch them win every time, like the Springboks from

SOUTH AFRICA, which is full of gold and diamonds and other Joellery, and exports the horns of geographical beestes such as the cheerful heartibeeste, and the hearty dirtibeeste, and the funny little beestibeeste ; the inhabitants being indistinguishable from other hardy Domineers except that they pretend to talk Dutch, clothe their feet in foot-sacks and tend to have a stoep.

CHAPTER III

INSCRUTABLE PLACES

I. *The East*

THE authors were gratified to find after the briefest attempt to scrutinise it that the East is, as everybody knows, Inscrutable.

They found, for example, that there is no generally known difference between China and Japan—except, of course, Manchuria ; that Thibet has deliberately refused to have any Geography at all (Bravo) and that Persia and Arabia are just one vast inscrutable Nomad's Land containing all the sand you can't find at Brighton.

II. *Russia*

A similar. attempt to scrutinise Russia, *and subsequently America*, led the authors to the same rather consoling conclusion : namely, that they are, for the present at least, *quite inscrutable*.

It is, however, just possible to distinguish between the Old Russia with its old capital, St. Petersberg, and the New Russia with its new capital, Petrograd, subsequently re-named Leningrad, or possibly Stalingrad, and likely to be re-named again and again every Five Years, according to Plan, as the country becomes progressively less and less retrograd.

The Old Russia was inhabited by fierce Cossacks, who (we are informed on all hands) roamed about rapidly dressed in stuffy Cassocks, and gentle peasants who moaned about stupidly (we are informed, on all fours) dressed in filthy *Samovars :* and both were totally devoted to Music (Russ. : Moujik) in the form of Balalaika bands, so called because each member played as he balalalaiked (Bravo !).

The New Russia, on the contrary, appears to be inhabited by ruthless Commissionaires, who control the Fûdkus (or ruthless Cominterns) and everything else including the rich or non-collectivised peasants (Kulaks) who are usually dead, and the collectivised or happy peasants (Kodaks) who tell no tales ; so that there is now no hope (Russ. : Nevskiprospekt) of scrutinising Russia in the old way (viz. steppe by steppe) and Russian Geography has therefore been, quite rightly, *suspended* altogether until it becomes safe to scrutinise it again.

SPECIAL APPENDIX ON INDIA
Part I. *Bother India*

India is really part of the Inscrutable East so that writers can, and mostly do, say anything they like about it, however inscrutable.

We will therefore state fearlessly that the climate of India is very hot (especially during the Hot Weather) ; and also rather cold (especially during the Cold Weather). For months no rain falls (during the Dry Weather) ; at other times nothing else falls (and this is called, with Oriental subtlety, the Wet Weather).

Sunset in India occurs with mysterious suddenness, and is succeeded at once by the mysterious Eastern *Night;* which is in turn brought savagely to an end by the pitiless Eastern *Day.*

And this has been going on, mysteriously, since time inscrutable. No one can stop it.

NOTE : The Thing which causes all the Wet Weather, climate, etc., in India is called *The Mongoose.* All depends on what this bothersome Thing is up to : whenever it gets the answer wrong (*Rongoose*) there are fearful thunderbursts, bunderbusts, etc. ; dams and irritation works are hastily started by the Government and the native soldiers commit Puttee to propitiate It. But nothing avails till The Mongoose gets itself into a favourable condition again (Bongoose).

RACIAL DISTINCTIONS

The inhabitants are divided roughly into two sections ; the Plain People belong to one rough section, and the Hill Tribes belong to another even rougher section, and are said to be even plainer (bad luck). The Hill Men are mostly Pythans, a sporting race of Moslems, armed with machine-guns, swords, knives, drain-pipes, etc.

Prominent among the people of the Plains are the Babus, an ingenious race of Hindus armed with higher-certificates, spinning-wheels, etc. They have very little self-control and are apt to swallow too much sugar-ghandi, after which they go hartaling about beating Chittagongs, Moslems, etc., in a distressingly non-co-operative manner.

As a result, most of India has to be controlled (like Russia) by Distracted Commissionaires, whose job gets harder and bahardur every year : but these are, of course, all pukka white men and therefore belong to

Part II. Pukka India

As everyone knows, the splendid officials (borough sahibs, etc.) of the Indian Civil Service live in dark bungalows and work so devotedly that they get punkah and punkah (especially during the Hot Weather) until they are compelled to retire to the Blackwoods of Cheltenham, where they secretly worship numberless small brass gods (lares et Benares) clad solely in tiger-skins and the insignia of the Most Eminent Order of the Star of India (bravo).

We consider ourselves, therefore, much honoured in being able to print the following accounts of the White Man's Boredom, from notes kindly supplied by Sir Pelteney Bludd-Bunderbust K.C.S.I. (failed G.C.I.E.), late Burra Surveyor of the disturbed district known as the Central Dacoit.

It appears, then, that the climate in C.D., as always in India, exercises a derisive influence : the Hot Weather being productive of a regrettable amount of *tiffin* between the wives of Officials (*memsahibs* or

" Intractables ") and their strong silent spouses (*mum-sahibs* or " Unteachables ") ; while the Cold Weather subjects most of these Residents to a very trying laryngeal affection known in the Central Dacoit as *koffin*, and also to the even more trying pharyngeal affliction known, even in England, as *Sniffin.*

The routine of the official day is unalterable : the official is called at six and after a hurried bath (*wallah*) dresses himself (*collah*) and is down at a quarter to eight for breakfast (*swallah*). Next comes work for his particular Department (*bluffin*) during which, owing to the heat (that is during the Hot Weather) he is obliged to keep himself pegging along by means of an occasional whiskey-and-soda (*spiffin*).

It is this heat, or, alternatively (during the Cold Weather), cold, which makes it impossible to do any work (bad luck) during the afternoon, and renders necessary absolute rest (*nuffin*) from 2.30 to 5 p.m. (This is the famous *I.C.S.ta*, which is also observed, in sympathy, at the India Office, Whitehall, Lond., Eng.).

To maintain physical fitness, and impress the Native Mind, a little tennis (*biffin*) is played between 5.30 and 7 p.m., or golf (*fluffin*), according to the prevailing mongoose.

After dinner (*stuffin*) followed by a cigarette (*Abdullah*) or a pipe (*puffin*), usually smoked on the verandà (*verandah*), and a couple of *plukkahs* of bridge, the official retires and is in bed (*pillah*) by 10.15, and by 10.30 (except in the Hot Weather) asleep—thank god (*Allah*).

MYTH-INFORMATION

Fig. i.   Bronze Statue of The Iron Duke in
Hyde Park.
A famous English Myth-representation

CHAPTER I

IMPORTANCE OF MYTHS

DURING the course of their investigations the
authors questioned a number of average
school-boys as to which educational subject
they considered the more important—MYTHS, or
MATHS. They answered, at once,—Moths.

When shown, however, an average number of canes,
and other forms of WOE, they all admitted (at once)

that there must have been some myth-under-standing . . .

The truth is, of course, that the importance of Myths cannot be exaggerated (bad luck).

Everyone knows that these splendid old legends of heroic times—the Myths of Hellas, the Tales of Asgard, the Arthurian Cycle—have inspired our Poets, Artists and Statesmen as (and when) nothing else has ; and that, as a result, we English have for generations been myth-construed, myth-represented and myth-governed.

Indeed, a stroll round the public squares of any large European town is enough to convince the stupidest investigator that all Western Culture is fundamentally myth-guided.

CHAPTER II

SOME PRACTICAL USES

Quite apart from inspiring Poets and Statesmen to every conceivable form of myth-behaviour, and educating everybody in Beauty, Woe and other classical amenities (see later), Myths have their everyday practical uses.

Where would you be, by Jove, (socially speaking), if you were not able to cap your County friends' cheery myth-quotations when strolling in the Paddock at Cowes or in the Royal Enclosure at Whipsnade ?

Or again. Supposing you had arranged to meet a young friend at the British Museum, by-Jove-what-a-bloomsbury-fool you would feel if you were to miss

her altogether owing to your inability to distinguish
between fig. ii—

and fig. iii—

*Fig. ii. Odysseus
bidding farewell
to the Hydro
(Praxiteles)*

*Fig. iii. Umslo-
pogas defying
the Erymanth-
ean Boer
(Isosceles)*

—or any of the other famous myth-shapen master-
pieces illustrated on pages 86–87.

CHAPTER III

RUTHLESS RUNES

" A Norse ! A Norse ! My kingdom for a Norse ! "
(Sleipner's Myth-translations from the Edda.)

BUT the thing which makes Myths of all kinds so
uplifting, compelling (and in practice compulsory) is
the moral and spiritual beauty which we can all find
in them—if we start young enough and refuse to take
Woe (or even Moths) for an answer.

Consider the grand old Outlandish Viking Songs, or
Sagas, about the MYTHICAL REALMS OF ASGARD, FISH-
GARD and MUDGARD.

These lovely old Norsery Tales have, like most

other myths, always been found exceptionally advisable as bed-time readings for little children—whose little nightmares are apt to be quite vague and formless in the absence of such handy myth-conceptions as REVENGEFUL RUNES, HIDEOUS DWARFS, BEREWOLVES and other spell-binding Scandinavian bric-à-brac ; and whose best little impulses respond at once to the lovely little idea of VALHALLA—the Viking HEAVEN in which the HEROES spend Eternity in the ECSTASY OF FURIOUS FIGHTING, SERIOUS DRINKING, ETC., while those unfortunate enough not to have been SLAIN IN BATTLE eke out eternal boredom in the far-off futile REALM OF PIFFELHEIM (bad luck).

CHAPTER IV

GOOD-KNIGHT STORIES

IN addition to their manly tone, the grand old pagan Sagas have the further recommendation of an almost complete lack of Norseous love-interest.

This unfortunately is not true of the totally Christian Myths of King Arthur and his splendid Knights ; in fact many investigators have concluded, after reading the Good Knight Sir Thomas Mallory's *Morte d'Arthur*, that the Rules of Chivalry entitled any young Sir to do any blessed thing he liked to any Blessed Damozel he happened to meet.

NOTE : *This is a ridiculous myth-interpretation of the facts ; on the contrary, by the laws of mediæval joustice he could do nothing to anybody without Power of A Tourney.*

Such mistakes are caused by a failure to realise that the Keynote of these beautiful mediæval romances is just sheer GLAMOUR, e.g. :

HOW AT A GREAT FEAST SIR DYNALOT BEHELD SIR
GLAMIS LE MONSTRE AND TOOK HIM FOR A DYNASOR
AND WOULD HAVE MADE DO A CARNAGE OF HIM FOR
HIGH GAME BUT WHEN HE KNEW HIM FOR A SCOTT
KNIGHT DID STRAIGHTWAY MAKE DO A PORRAGE OF
HIM FOR A DAMOZEL.

LOVE IN A MYTH

A brief research among the Poets will convince
anyone that in this epoch the women of the upper
classes (and a few Beggar Maids) were all bewitchingly
beautiful and that most of the Heroines of these
enthralling Romances were rather *Belles Dames Sans
Fairy Ann.*

But that was not their fault because, as everyone
knows, they all had the misfortune to quaff love-
lotions (or -poultices) which ensured their being permanently in love with *The Wrong Knight*—thus
obliging any other really noble-minded Knight (*a*) to
slay their husbands and (*b*) to burn his own wife alive
(*noblesse oblige*) if he had any reason to suspect that
she had recently quaffed a love-poultice in which he
was not mentioned.

But this is not the sort of thing that anyone (except
peradventure a totally unbridled Troubadour) would
wish to harp on : *the Glamour is the thing, e.g.*

OF THE LOVE OF DAME TREMULEUSE LA BLANCHE
MANGE FOR A LOATHLY WORM HIGHT PADDINGTON
THAT PURSUED A BISHOP FIVE LEAGUES FOR THE
INTENT TO HAVE TOASTED HIM IN PARTIBUS AND
HOW HAPLY SHE WAS CURED OF HER DOATING WEAK-
NESSE AND HAD GREAT JOY OF SIR PALLEAS LE BOLSTRE
AND WAS THERETOBY SUFFOLCATED   (bad luck).

If not yet surfeited with Glamour, note carefully

Fig. iv

Fig. iv, mythical object discovered at Glastonbury and identified by the authors as the Arthurian Cycle. Notice (A) The Siege Perilous, (B) Excalibrake, (C) Gothic wheel-form. It was apparently steered by faith (or witchcraft).

CHAPTER V

WHEN GREEK MEETS GREEK

But for sheer concentrated Beauty, Glamour and Inspiration there is nothing like the grand old classical Myths of Ancient Greece.

Fig. v. " The Wrath
of Achilles "

For instance, everyone knows that British boys are bound to become absolute Barbarians (or possibly even Bulgarians) unless they are periodically ducked in the Pierian Springs of Greek Culture and held under until they admit the beauty of such memorable legends as—e.g.

(A) THE LOVELY STORY OF JASON AND MEDEA

Part I.

Medea, daughter of Aeëtes (or Eäetes) King of Aëa (or Eäe), became enamoured of Jason (or Iason)—son of Aeson (or Eaëason) King of Aëïöü—when he came to fetch the Golden Fleece from her father.

NOTE : The Golden Fleece was a Fleece (or Fleäece) made of gold which was doomed by Fate to be fetched (by Jason).

Having fetched the Fleece, Jason fled with Medea in a small boat accompanied by Medea's small brother Absyrtus.

The father of Medea pursued them, however (on the other hand, in another boat, other things being equal, etc.). Medea therefore made a *beautiful plan*. She

Fig. vi. Odysseus about to offer wine to the Cyclops

Fig. vii. Odysseus, wine having been offered

took her small brother Absyrtus and CUT HIM INTO SMALL BEAUTIFUL ABSYRD PIECES, which she strewed in the wake of the boat with the object of detaining her father. In this she was entirely successful, her father stopping his boat and spending day after day in mid-ocean trying to fit the small absyrd pieces together in order to see whom they would make.

End of Part I.

Part II.

Meanwhile Jason's half-beautiful half-uncle Pelias had seized the throne of Æson, or possibly caused it to be seized ; and put Aeson to the sword, or much more probably caused the sword to be put Aeson.

In order to seize the throne back again and present it to Jason, Medea now thought of another plan, which is probably *the most beautiful plan in all Mythology*.

She deceived the daughters of Pelias, and CAUSED THEM TO CUT THEIR AGED FATHER INTO A THOUSAND EQUAL PIECES (OR PEÄECES) AND BOIL HIM IN A CAULDRON. This, she assured them, would restore him to youth and beauty.

But when Pelias had been cut up and boiled he *looked just as old and ugly as ever* (bad luck). Jason was thus so disappointed that he deserted Medea and caused himself to marry Alopetia, daughter of Perispomenon and half-cousin of the beautiful Periscopë who gave birth to twin serpents with the feet of fire-breathing she-goats.

End of Part II.

Part III.

Having consulted the Fates, Furies, Harpies and other beauties of Ancient Greece, Medea took a final and totally beautiful revenge on Jason by MURDERING ALL HER OWN CHILDREN, and fleeing to Athens in a chariot drawn by twin-Dragons with the fire-breathing feet of mythical he-hens. . . .

End of lovely story of Jason and Medea.

(B) THE NOBLE STORY OF PERSEUS

Perseus was the son of Zeus and Danäe and the grandson of Proposteros and (according to one authority) the great-grandson of Properiposteros, the twin-brother of Pontresina, who LAID POISONED EGGS on the twin walls of Thebes or (according to another authority) twin eggs on the poisoned walls, and was consequently turned by Zeus into an ostrich.

Fig. viii.
The English
Myth

Warned in a dream that he was DOOMED TO PERISH at the hands of his grandson, Proposteros TURNED INTO A BAD MAN and incarcerated Danäe and the little Perseus in a very small Oracle, which he then hurled into the sea, and in which Mother and Son (or according to a few romantic authorities *the twain*) floated helplessly until they were TURNED INTO PORPOISES by Zeus and finally picked up on the island of Cerebos by Dactyl, an ignorant fisherman, who ignorantly suckled them for 19 years and was then quickly turned into a geranium by Apollo Bomphilogeranios.

Meanwhile Pterodactyl, King of Cerebos, fell in 'ove with Danäe, or (according to a more cautious authority) became enamoured (of her, understood); but, not being in the least enamoured of Perseus, sent him away to fetch the MEDUSA'S HEAD in the hope that it would turn him into something.

Happening, during the journey, to meet the three beautiful daughters of Sago, who happened to have the bodies of SAVAGE SWANS, and ONE TOOTH and ONE EYE between them which they borrowed from one another when they wanted to sing, Perseus seized (*a*) the Eye, thus rendering himself invisible, and (*b*) the Tooth, thus rendering himself indigestible, and then attacked the Medusa : but discovered that WHENEVER HE LOOKED AT HER HE WAS TURNED INTO A STONE (bad luck). He therefore looked at her reflection in a mirror and cut that off instead.

On his way home Perseus found a special sort of nymph tied to a rock, and on being told that it was An Dromedary, easily untied and married her.

The rest of the story is almost unbearably beautiful.

Perseus, arriving at Cerebos, turned the Wicked King Pterodactyl and all his friends into stone, and compelled the ignorant Dactyl to stop being a geranium and become ignorantly King of Cerebos instead.

Finally he went in pursuit of his grandfather Proposteros, and according to an excessively beautiful tradition accidentally SMOTE HIM TO DEATH while HURLING THE DISH-CLOTH at the Olympic Games, in revenge for which the Goddess Athene made him immortal every seven years, and turned him into a twin egg, and compelled An Dromedary to marry a TWIN-DIPLODOCUS WITH THE FIRE-QUENCHING FEET OF MYTH-ICAL TIN-HYDRANTS.

Fig. ix.

N.B. Fig. ix represents a beautiful Coin struck in the face by King Euphrates. Also believed to be a medal presented to himself by Perseus after he had turned everybody he could think of into stone (origin of Greek Art).

MYTH RECONSTRUCTION BY PROF. JOHN REYNOLDS

▰▰. Original stone.
···· Conjectural.

MUCH BETTER RECON-
STRUCTION BY THE
AUTHORS

SPACE FOR ABSOLUTELY
SPLENDID RECONSTRUC-
TION BY THE READER

VIII

THE TRUTH ABOUT BIRDS

CHAPTER I

OBJECT OF BIRDS

THE Authors' Researches in this field confirm the opinion of all the best Manuals and Primers on Birds and Bird Watching; namely, that the chief practical use of Birds is to teach people HOW TO GO ABOUT WITH THEIR EYES OPEN.

How valuable and practical that lesson is can only be realised by those who, like ourselves, have made the scientific experiment of going about for days on end WITH THEIR EYES TIGHTLY SHUT.

The results were striking: we found ourselves continually gate-crashing, rubbing shoulders with the grate, running into everybody up the wrong way—

while experiencing all the time a mysterious sensation *almost akin to blindness.*

This then is the chief or Primery Use of Birds. But there are others (in case the first fails) : you can, for instance, preserve birds in thickets and then shoot them ; or you can shoot them in buckets and then preserve them ; or you can stuff them into cages without shooting them, or shoot them into cages without stuffing them, and so on. . . .

One way or another you can nearly always kill them in the end, and eat them ; or even, if you prefer it, kill them without eating them—though you cannot, unfortunately, eat them without killing them (bad luck).

NOTE : Many people think it is cruel to preserve birds for months merely for the pleasure of *shooting them in the end,* but in our opinion it makes very little difference where you shoot them.

Similarly as regards *stuffing ;* some people think it is cruel to geese to stuff their livers into *pâté de foie gras,* while others think it is cruel to people to stuff *pâté de foie gras* into their livers. In our opinion there is practically nothing to choose between stuffed birds and stuffed people.

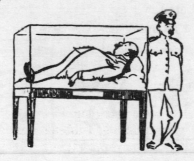

Of course, it is possible that all this snuffing and stuffing does not appeal to you at all : in that case there are plenty of other useful things you can do with Birds : for instance, you can collect their eggs and press them carefully in an album as you would wild moths or antique beetles ; or you can train them to nest in your hand, or beard ; or if you really *like* them you can go down to the river and play ducks and drakes with them—but of course only with the *flat* ones, such as the common flat-catcher, the plat-billed duckibus, or the greater crested muffin.

CHAPTER II

STRUCTURE OF BIRDS AND OF THEIR EGGS

THE structure of birds is not really very complicated : they are constructed for the most part of *warm bunches of brownish feathers* with two cold slithy legs placed at right angles to it all (see Fig. i). The two longest bunches are (i) the *wings*, which are so called because the bird flies with them (cf. " winging its way," " on the wing," " wings of a dove "), and (ii) the *tail*, so called because it is the last part of the bird, judged from the front (cf. " Tail-piece," " Heads or Tails," " Tail of a Shirt," etc.).

STRUCTURE OF BIRD

Fig. i.

There are only *two legs* (bad luck) but each of them has 4 *toes*, three in front and a spare one at the back in case it is wanted ; and right in front of the bird there is *one* very important *beak*, or combined mouth, nose, teeth, moustache, etc.

As for birds' eggs, they are all *ovoid*, i.e. egg-shaped, which is fairly consoling ; and as a consequence all birds are avoid, i.e. bird-shaped. (These scientific terms are unovoidable). It follows inevitably that there are *no square eggs* since there are no square birds to lay them (jolly bad luck).

Now that you have learnt all you know about the structure and right use of Birds, you are ready to introduce yourself to the most exclusive Bird-watching circles (see fig. ii, Bird watching Circles ; also fig. ii, Bird watching circles).

Fig. ii (also Fig. ii)

CHAPTER III

FIELD WORK

ONCE you start Bird-watching yourself,* you will of course go in for what is called Field-Work.

But in England, remember, *you can't do that in a field* —even with your eyes wide open.

NOTE : This is because of the proprietors of the Comic Papers, whose livelihood depends so much upon (i) the IRATE FARMER shouting hither and thither, with his mouth wide open and (ii) the inconsolable BULLS leaping from knoll to tussock, with their horns and noses wide open.

So you will probably make for The Woods. And here, just as you are about to discover the answer to such time-honoured conundrums, or cross-bird puzzles, as *Do Woodcock carry their Young ?* or *Should Woodchough drink their wood-fluff ?* or *How much wood would a Woodchuck chuck, if an etcetera ?* you will be interrupted (in England) by an IRATE PHEASANT, who will remind you that (in England) TRESPASSERS WILL BE PROSECUTED and that he will have the law on you for disturbing the game-keepers during the matey season.

Keep smiling (or some absolutely General Knowledge of that sort) : sooner or later you will realise the *Whole Truth* about Bird-watching which you discovered long ago in your own back garden, namely—

(i) That most birds are Rooks or Sparrows (bad luck). You will never get a Diploma for watching these.

(ii) That the really genuine *ornithological* birds, i.e. the bannocks, bludgeons, gadgets, fidgets, pipwits, trollopes and lesser crusted crumpets

* See Fig. ii again ; Bird-watching yourself.
  Also Fig. ii ; Bird watching yourself.

are quite indistinguishable from one another,* and that long before you can focus your field-glasses on them they *migrate*. . . .

CHAPTER IV

BIRD SONGS

To be honest, the best Manuals make it pretty clear that Bird-watching is mostly done, contrary to expectation, *with the ears*. So perhaps the best thing to do next would be to try again and start going about this time *with your ears wide open*.

All the same, you will know all the time that when you have listened with a good deal of rapture to the " *lively chirrup* of the *Pip-pippet*, as it flops from branch to branch " (see " How to Win the Bird-Badger's Badge," by a Scout Warden), and to the " *metallic alarm-note* (or *cheerful shurrup*) of the *Back-chat*," you will be compelled to admit that *the only bird whose song can be identified for certain is the Swan*.

This is, of course, done by watching the bird singing ; if the bird dies at the end, then you know it was a Swan.

Many enthusiastic watchers maintain that it is easy to recognise " the *loud whirrup* of the *Whoopoee*, which is emitted incessantly for two or three weeks on the approach of weasels, weevils, moths, otters, drome-daries or other vermin."

It is not so easy as you might think. Actually, there is no guarantee that the sound was not emitted by a

* With the notable exception of the rare Scottish Ptarmagant or Sporting Ghilliecrailzie, which distinguishes itself by growing white feathers in the winter in order to conceal the snow

Starling, since "*the starling can imitate the calls of all birds with extraordinary exactness*" (see "Bird-Sanctuaries" by A Bird-Verger, and all accepted authorities).

And borrows their plumage, too, no doubt, and goes about in it laying their eggs. In fact, it is an important rule that *in case of doubt the answer is probably a starling*.

CHAPTER V

"WHY BIRDS SING"

It is very difficult to determine the *exact meanings* of the various calls, cries, hoots, booms, thumps, yodels, and yiffle-yaps which birds emit; because different birds make the same noise for different reasons, and the same birds make different noises for the same reason —and so on, for different reasons.

Some birds such as the Battle-cock (fem. Shuttle-hen) sing when they are startled; others such as the Dumtit are startled when they sing. Generally speaking, birds sing because they are *excited*. The excitement, of course, may be due to the bird being *happy* (possibly because it is its birthday), or to its being *angry* (because it has laid a hard-boiled egg, or seen itself incorrectly reported in a newspaper), or to its being *in love*, or *in doubt*, or possibly *in debt* (being unable to pay its bill). Or again it may be just due to its being *excited*.

This much at any rate is known, that "*when Jays are happy they scream*," and that "*when the Diver is in love it screams like a child in great terror.*" It is therefore as well to know the breeding-times of such birds, so that when you hear a scream like a child in great terror you will know whether it is a Diver "in the interesting but short-lived court-ship phase," or just an uninteresting and probably short-lived child in great terror.

Such knowledge has saved many a keen bird-lover an unnecessary detour when strolling near the banks of a weir or mill-race.

On the whole, after watching as many birds as we could find (till our ears ached) we are inclined to the belief that most birds *have no idea* why they utter such a variety of chortles, tootles, twiddles and other twaddles and that many of them are not even aware they are doing it.

And anyway (as Professor Whangus Macabre, late Prof. of Moral Ferocity, University of Aberdour, says) it is dangerous to probe the licentious mysteries of the ornithogeneric pandemonium, and (as Prof. de Nonchalant of Tarascon says) it does not matter in the least since (as Aristotle argued in 340 B.C.) it is impossible to legislate against the cuckoo, and (as Plato quickly said before him) their songs will continue to be birdsongs especially in relation to their virtue as song-birds, or even in virtue of their relation to the songs of birds.

. . . Nay, but by Zeus, someone will say——
Cuckoo to all that, let's go and look for birdsnests.

CHAPTER VI

BIRDSNESTS

IF you could believe the books written by bird-nudgers, egg-snobs and other Seasonal Pests, it would appear that birds are prepared to build their nests anywhere, e.g. in the Breeches of Obsolete Canons, in the depths of ear-trumpets, or even in the pockets of golf bags during a remorseless " holeing out " on the 18th green.

Fortunately, we are now able to reveal *The Truth about Birdsnests*, too, in a brace of short never-to-be-forgotten Birdsnesting Rules, which our Researches have proved to be *Absolutely General Knowledge*.

(i) *The only birds which really build nests are Blackbirds, Sparrows and Thrushes (or Blackbirds).*

(ii) It is an extraordinary but indisputable fact that *whereas an enormous number of these birds built nests last year, practically none have built nests this year.*

Or is there some antiquarian bird which *builds old nests ?*

The answer to that question is *not* General Knowledge : the question itself, however, leads inevitably to

CHAPTER VII

BAD HABITS OF BIRDS

BIRDS are not only fowl : in some respects they are quite horrid—especially in their *habits*.

For one thing, they fug : they persist in going to sleep with their heads buried in their feathers, although they must know that it is very bad for them not to have plenty of fresh air.

Another thing : if you watch birds carefully, you will see them poking their heads in and out of their left and right breast pockets and then, having failed to find their handkerchiefs, *wiping their noses on the branches.* All birds do this. It is disgusting.

Again, birds *sleep all night with their eyes open* (Chaucer says so), which is unsporting, as it means that the anxious Bird-Watchers who sit up and watch them can't tell when they are asleep and when they aren't and write their books all wrong in consequence.

This problem is intensified by another bad habit amongst birds, viz., *talking in bed ;* although possibly pardonable in nightingales, nightjars, nightcaps and various kinds of owls (which, it seems, *sing in their sleep* owing to some kind of inhibition or possibly indigestion), the habit is obviously inexcusable amongst partridges, corncrakes and sparrows, all of which deliberately laugh and " squeak and gibber " all through the day and then proceed to cough and gibber and mutter all through the night.

The result is that they grossly oversleep themselves in the morning and are still fast asleep (*with their eyes still wide open*) when the Bird-watchers come round to call them with the early morning worm.

And when these birds (sparrows especially) do get up, they are so dazed with sleep that *they bath in the wrong places*, sometimes in the BIRD WATER put out by thoughtful old ladies for them to drink, or in the (clearly marked) DOG DISH, or sometimes just in the dirt and dust at the roadside in full view of anyone who happens to be passing.

Later in the day, they go back to the old lady's garden and *drink the bath water* out of the clearly-marked BIRD-BATH.

And need one mention the malignant behaviour of owls, which hide (even after dark) in hollow tree-trunks, and hoot at strangers for no reason at all, and *won't come out?*

Moreover, in conclusion, could one think of anything more apposite, or composite, to quote than the famous Bird-song from Shakespeare (*Nothing Much To Do About Anything*—Act XXI, Scene XXII, lines 6793–end)?

TIT-BITTERN

Eena Meena Myna Mo
(Sing hullo, sing dynamo)
Catch a tit-wit by its toe—
(Silly, silly dynamo)
If it yodels let it go—
It's not a tit-wit. No!

Ah ! No—
(Tell it so)
Heed not then its pretty tweeting
(If 'tis goose, say Bo !)
Journeys end in plovers meeting
(If 'tis raven—Poe !)
Let go, let go !
Once bittern, woe !
Heigh-ho,
Heigh nonny no,
Heigh nonny nonny nonny nonny . . .

> *Buckets without. Enter King*
> *Penguin with Girl Guides,*
> *Game-keepers, Egg-watchers,*
> *and two Obsolete Canons. A*
> *Peal of Ordnance. The King*
> *lays an Egg. Sensation.*

APPENDIX

SOME LITTLE-KNOWN BIRDS AND THEIR WORST HABITS

The Slotted Bag-Snatcher : lays its eggs upwards
(three at a time) from underneath the nest. Very clever.
A bird to watch.

The Australasian Cooee Bird : a tail-less finch which
emits an irritating call when lost and (having no wings,
partner) *flies with its feet.* This is, of course, wrong.

The Plat-billed Duckibus : has spines in its feet and
its feet on its back (bad luck) : it therefore walks
upside-down and is thus in every way invertebrate.

The Lesser Snousel or *Dream-warbler :* goes to sleep
while flying and thus migrates to the wrong country.
On arrival moults in the Dog-Bath. A worthless fowl.

ORNITHOBLIOGRAPHY

Hand-book on Birds . .	by Two in a Bush
To Wit to Woo . . .	by A Married Owl
A Bag's-Eye View of Birds .	by A Poacher
Number Engaged . . .	by A Low Buzzard
One Good Tern . . .	by Another
Once Bittern . . .	by A Retired Bird-Watcher
Love me Love my Peacock .	by Thomas Love Peacock
Memoirs of a Wasted Life .	by A Nut-hatch
Just as I Feared . .	by Geo. Bernard Shaw

Read also periodically :—

Chiff-Chaff	daily ½d.
Stonechat	monthly 2/6d.

IX

PHOTOCRAFT

A BRIEF EXPOSÉ OF MODERN PHOTOGRAPHY

CHAPTER I

INTRODUCTORY

THERE are two spools of thought in photo-graphy. People with stern but sedentary impulses favour the form of nerve-test known as Sitting for your Portrait, while actively courageous people prefer the more heroic kind of photography which makes big demands on you such as " *Bring Back Your Holiday In Sparkling Snapshots Which Will Never Go Bald.*" We will focus first upon the former.

CHAPTER II

APRÈS DAGUERRE FINI

IN the hardy old days of the *Daguerreotype*, Professional Portraiture meant being guerrotted-by-numbers in front of a louring Highland landscape ; which easily accounts for the strong expressions of despair so frequently recorded and for the fervour with which, after the ceremony, all joined hands and sang the old photo-chanty which begins " *Après Daguerre fini . . .*"

Nowadays, Professional Portraiture is conducted in a clinical, rather than penal atmosphere.

The Subject (or " sitter " as an easy case is called) is first *Hypnotised* (free) by a totally consoling typist-receptionist, and when sufficiently sub-conscious, lured into a Whited Sepulchre and *Hoodwinked* (for 100 gns.) by an Eminent Scientist disguised as a Royal Academician. All of which may account for

Daguerrotted   Passportout

the expressions of Peter-Panchromatic inanity with which the bottom drawer of your bureau is now stuffed.

There is also, of course, a cheaper kind of Portraiture which the Foreign Secretary is compelled to sign and frame, free, for 10/6 and which is called *passeportout* and enables travellers to pass anywhere unrecognised.

Finally, there are some rather cowardly devotees of professional photography who prefer *grouping themselves* together in small herds of Banqueting Buffaloes, Old Boys, Hon: Incorporated Plesiosauri or other publicly exhibitable fossils, and merging their personalities in the group-consciousness to such an extent that each Old Buffalo gets reduced literally to a cipher.

CHAPTER III

THE REAL THING

BUT all this is *tame* compared with the really instructive *character-building* practice of Taking Up Amateur Photography, which, as we suggested above, makes BIG DEMANDS on you.

Mere snapshotting is not enough. The genuine amateur photographer *does everything himself:* he loads the camera himself, *sub rosa*, in some shady corner of the garden, unloads it again distrustfully, loads it again with the film back to front, points the camera at the cat, waits for the sun to emerge from behind a cloud, unpoints the camera, points it at the puppy, the wife, the welkin, etc., and finally presses at least one of the levers. After that he plunges into a dark-room to develop the picture, unplunges indefatigably into the sunlight to print it, enlarge it, reduce it, stick it in, unstick it, stick it in straight, unstick himself, stick-whack the puppy if the latter has taken up photography, too, and won't put it down. . . .

No photographer, in fact, is worth his sodium till he has done all these things again and again, until he has become hardened by prolonged exposure and has learnt to take the rough with the glossy.

NOTE : The amateur will also be wise to get himself inoculated against HYPOPHOBIA, since, when attacked by this terrible disorder the dark-room worker suddenly sees red, something goes snap in his brain, he drains the Hypo dish at a gulp, and then, obsessed by an *idée fixe*, goes reeling and rolling about till he falls finally between two spools and is squeegeed out of all recognition.

CHAPTER IV

HOCUS-FOCUS

THE master word of photography is, of course, *focus*. But there is nothing in that : it is only the photographic word for distance, being derived, as everyone knows, from the Latin word meaning 'hearth and home' (c.f. "Far from the old focus at home"— *Homer*).

For instance, in taking "close-ups" the most important rule is that the eyes should be properly focussed (see fig. i).

Right   **Wrong**

Fig. i

But the chief thing to remember about focus is that everything is sharp at 100 ft. or Infinity. So, if your sweetheart has rather fuzzy features it is best to put her as far away from the camera as possible, say at Infinity.

There are many other tricks of the trade which can be used to conceal defects in the sitter's features: *bald heads* can be concealed by careful aiming of the camera (see fig. ii) : *double chins* by halving the exposure.

Fig. ii   Fig. iii

(Or, of course, wigs, false beards, etc., can be employed.)

The defect in fig. iii can be got over by the use of a wide-angle lens or blue spectacles, and extreme obesity by taking plenty of exercise. In a case of bald head, double chin, squint *and* extreme obesity it is best to take the portrait from behind or preferably in a fog, or even total darkness (see Appendix—*Infra-Dig Photography*).

N.B. There is *no* photographic cure for asthma (bad luck).

CHAPTER V

HINTS FOR BEGINNERS

I. When setting out on a photographic holiday *always provide yourself with two cameras*, one to leave in the train going and the other to leave in the cab coming back.

II. *Specialise.* Most of the best *genres* are already overdone, but we can never forget the case of Col. ——, who, becoming confused as to which of the camera's two "eyes," the photograph gets in at, the plain or the red one, spent the whole of his first photographic tour photographing his own V.P. Upon it

becoming known, however, that Col. ——'s album was the only album in the world devoted entirely to photographs of one Vest Pocket, Col. —— immediately became famous, and, as a result of his picture (with Vest Pocket inset) appearing in the newspapers, he received numerous attractive offers of marriage, and soon after became a Director of several photographic firms.

III. *Do not make the mistake of trying to load the camera yourself on the first occasion.* Afte following the instructions for a few hours you will be come entangled, strangled and slightly mangled and will have to be taken to the nearest chemist and reversed, unfixed, washed, dried and generally trimmed-up and toned-down before being sent out again into the great open spaces.

CHAPTER VI

PHOTO FAME

WHATEVER happens, however many times you make an April Spool of yourself, do not be disheartened. Keep snapping : in the end you will become so good that you will be able to go back to your old school and *lecture with lantern slides* made from the snaps you took in Egypt. It must be *Egypt*, because it has been proved that all schoolboys can recognise the Pyramids *even in an Old Boy's snapshot.*

This will be one of the proudest moments of your life as an Old Boy : but keep your head—and, above all, *keep the picture of your dragoman till the very end.* Because whenever a lecturer says "This was our Dragoman—he didn't know he was being taken " the lantern man invariably puts on one of the King, upside down, whereupon the audience stands up and sings ' God save the King.'

Even if they stand up upside down and sing ' God save the King ' backwards, do not be discouraged ; the great snapshot pioneer, Lord Kodak, was never discouraged by anything, not even when he showed his first Kodak to the Emperor Napoleon and the latter only muttered " *C'est magnifique, mais ce n'est pas Daguerre !* "

APPENDIX

STOP-PRESS-BUTTON NEWS

Latest Developments

Owing to recent discoveries it is now possible to photograph everything, however invisible, or even undesirable, at any distance, at any time of the day or night, and to publish the result in a newspaper.

There are, for instance, the new special `*Ilfra-red plates* (actuated by *ultra-sensitive infra-fog rays*) which enable you to take photographs *in a fog* and are obviously very useful, because if you were having a

bath (say, in some *Ilfracombe digs*) on a foggy day and
the bathroom window wouldn't shut and the fog came
in—or, say, if the window wouldn't open and the
steam couldn't get out—and you *couldn't find the soap*
and you began to feel *ultra-sensitive* and *red* and *infra-
dig* and altogether utterly beastly, and you decided
that it was very important to finish your bath and be
all right again—then by means of these *Ilfra-fog*
plates *you could take a photograph of the bathroom* and
look at the photograph and so find the soap and finish
your bath and, say, get down to dinner without getting
infra-combed or, to say the worst, *outfra-duck*, or
anything else that we wouldn't like to say.

Or again, there is the Long-Focus-Lens with *red
sensitive filter, ultra-big rays*, etc., which enables you
to take *extra-big* photographs, digs, etc., miles and
miles away. So, say we were all in Clapham together
(*in ultra-marine wigs*) and a hen (possibly even a *supra-
red hen* with *extra-long legs*) was flying over the S. Pole
and we read about it in the Evening Papers—then we
could take some of these Wrong-Focus Photographs
of it and send them to the newspapers and cut them
out afterwards and put them in our albums and show
them to people and feel absolute *supra-dogs*, and go
about singing the new Photo-chanty which begins—

> " Hocus-Focus, Filter and Ray,
> Take you by night, or take you by day,
> Or take you a thousand miles away
> With a hocus-focus, filter and ray."

TEST PAPER

ON

ABSOLUTELY GENERAL KNOWLEDGE

Time allowed—5 Minutes

1. How are you ?
2. *Who* are you ?
3. *Who gave you that name ?*
4. (*a*) Can you give us the right time ? Or
   (*b*) Are you a stranger in these parts yourself ?
   (N.B. Candidates marked with an asterisk may
   use the india-rubber.)
5. What are you doing now ?
6. (i) What would you like to do next ?
    (ii) Have you done it ?
    (iii) What are you thinking about now ?
7. " Father & Mother had I none, but that man's
   father was my father's fag at Oxford." *What do
   you know about that !*
8. (*a*) If there were ten horses in for a race and you
   burned your boots and put your shirt on the
   favourite and said you would eat your hat if it
   didn't come in first and it came in last and they
   couldn't get the shirt off and you'd left your hat
   in the cloak-room . . . (*b*) Are you attending ?
9. Would you like to stop now ? (If so, (i) hand in
   your paper if you have written anything on it, and
   (ii) tear up your blotting-paper if you have drawn
   anything silly on it.)
10.* (*a*) Have you got nice physical features ? If so,
    (*b*) Are you doing anything this evening ?

* For women-candidates only.

X

GOLLIWOLOGY

(Very difficult : Dictionaries may be useless)

I. GOLLIWOLAPOLOGY

GOLLIWOLOGY is not yet Absolutely General Knowledge.

Therefore—

Take any 8 schoolmasters you know, fold them up neatly 4×2 and stuff them right away in the left top-hand bottom drawer for ever.

Caution ! At the points where the vertical and horizontal lines of the Norfolk Jacket intersect, insert naphtha balls by rule of thumb, sideways (or, if slide-rules may be used, slideways).

II. BEGIN GOLLIWOLOGISING HERE

Now :

The sphere of Golliwology eludes all definition, though up to a point it overlaps with Gowology and of course with Golliwoliwology,—*or could if it wanted to* (see fig. i).

For instance, if a straight line is the shortest dis-

Fig. i

tance between two points, a circle (in Golliwology) is
the longest distance between the same point—*provided
the circle is big enough.*

Therefore—

Draw a simply enormous circle.

Now, where is the *point ?*

Gone.—You can't see it. That is what always
happens in Golliwology : the point continually eludes
you.

We must take something without any point in it at
all.

Take the Universe.

No, *you* take it.

Have you got it ? All right—

Space is curved but finite, and, as Einstein warned
the world, *if you go on you'll only bump into the back of
your own head.*

Therefore—

Take an infinite number of Scientists and bang them
to atoms. As the sparks fly upward, see fig. ii.

Years ago Balbus was General Knowledge. He
came right at the beginning of Education ; had nothing
to build on ; but Balbus made good.

Balbus built a wall (see fig. iii).

You don't see the point ? Of course not : the point

Fig. ii

Fig. iii

about Balbus is The Wall. And in Golliwology you're
up against it : *you've got your back to the wall.*

Besides, the wall is gone : it was turned Latin ages
ago, by almost everybody.

Therefore—

Creep back into the schoolroom at dawn . . .

Take down the first two Rs you thought of, and roll
them into one. You are left with a Rithmetic—and
the *Mystery Man* . . .

For instance—

" A Man makes a round rectangular box, without a
lid, 4 inches thick, and 2 inches wide, and turns it
upside-down. . . ." *Why does he do that ? What is he
thinking of ? What in the name of Golliwology will The
Man do next ?*

You can't tell (without a lid). You're furious (without a doubt). All right, then ;—just for the sake of a
bad-tempered argument—

(*a*) let x = The Answer

Therefore—

What is it ?

Ans. It's utterly unfair. Quite right : it's totally
marsupial. Therefore—

(*b*) let bygones be bygones

Or, if you're still furious—

Let bygones be bygones be bygones be bygones. (See
Figs. iv.)

Figs. iv

And now you are getting to the end of your tether. . . .

Wind yourself up again, therefore, backwards and inwards—that is, *spirally* towards the peg.

(*And Now You Are Getting To The End Of Your Writing-pad : In Re-ordering Insist On Dream-wove Marsupial Brand.*)

Face about, next, if you like, and follow your nose , *but don't waste time nosing about and following your face.*

Take any 8 figs that are left, fold them up neatly 4×2 and lump them together. (See Figs. v, vi, vii, viii, ix, x, xi, xii. . . . etc.)

Figs. v, vi . . . etc.

Lastly, and rather leastly, close the schoolroom door behind you ; shake away for ever the lumber you first thought of ; *and creep back to bed silently without waking the children.* . . .

MYSTERY P.S.

FAIR WARNING TO THE GENERAL

Caviar ! Do not attempt this Part. There is Latin lying Unseen in it which will almost certainly be Greek to you. *Caviar !*

By Order, By Gemini, etc.

Having already conducted some slightly unheard-of Researches into the question of what Things are Memorable and what are not, the authors were not entirely taken by surprise (though entirely flattered) when, shortly after the publication of " 1066 And All That," people with a keen sense of Rumour began attempting to father that histerical book upon one of the few *Punch* writers whose name and existence everybody feels absolutely certain about, namely, Mr. A. P. Herbert (Author of " Trial by Topsy," " Riverside up," etc.).

Our own absurd and unhystorical names, these people pointed out, were obviously mere *nom de plumage*, assumed by the downy water-gypsophiler for a whimsy.

And so like Shakespeare and Homer and Edward Lear we discovered that after a desperate attempt to become memorable we had only succeeded in becoming non-existent (bad luck—especially for " A.P.H.").

Happily we are able to save our Bacon from the painful necessity of making a Misleading Case of us and condemning us both, as Pretenders, to Tantitivate for life in the Tower of London.

We can submit powerful proof of our existence (you see later).

But before doing that we wish to appeal to all real modern authors to assist us in our great educational project by coming forward and making a clean breast of themselves and, in short, clearing up some of the Doubt and Mystery which surrounds their identities.

Punch writers in particular seem to delight in confusions, regardless of the trouble they give to educators such as ourselves. Take the famous Knox Mysteries. At first there appeared to be a simple constellation of *twin-brothers* (a sort of Equi-Knox), but later a *Father Knox* was observed ; and now even cool Bullett-headed writers like Gerald Baring Gould (" Maurice " for short) are quite benighted and go about muttering things like " *Knox et praeterea Knihil* " and " the path of glory leads but to the Graves."

And then " Evoe " (believed by so many romantic readers to be the lost tenth Muse)—what can he be ? What but a *Lucas a non lucendo* ?

And this " A.A." business. Why, when we were all *Ever So Young*. . . . And the Wyndhams Lewis. . . . And all this *Searching* for Deutero-Beachcomber. . . .

Don't they *want* to become memorable . . . ?

.   .   .   .   .   .

And now for the unanswerable proof of our own existence.

THE PROOF

It is recorded that when *Edward Lear* heard it conclusively proved by two ladies in a railway carriage that he was non-existent, and that his Nonsense Books had obviously been written by *Edward Earl* of Derby, he proved that he was more than a mere anagram by doffing his hat and showing his name on the lining.

We append, accordingly, our own unanswerable Hat, in facsimile, in the hope that you will find it utterly memorable and convincing

Memorable Hat (*Copyright if you can*)

So there!

Signed, by kind permission of Scotland Yard, Shakespeare, A. P. Homer, Mr. Haddock, and the Sanjak of Novibazar

W.C.S. & Y.